THE ANCIENT GREEKS IN 100 FACTS

PAUL CHRYSTAL

AMBERLEY

Paul Chrystal was educated at the universities of Hull and Southampton where he took degrees in Classics. His MPhil thesis was on attitudes to women in the poetry of the Roman love poets.

First published 2017

Amberley Publishing
The Hill, Stroud
Gloucestershire, GL5 4EP

www.amberley-books.com

British Library Cataloguing in Publication Data.
A catalogue record for this book is available from the British Library.

ISBN 978 1 4456 5642 7 (paperback)
ISBN 978 1 4456 5643 4 (ebook)

Typeset in 11pt on 13pt Sabon.
Origination by Amberley Publishing.
Printed in the UK.

Contents

INTRODUCTION

Who were the ancient Greeks? What was ancient Greece? Indeed, where exactly was ancient Greece and what happened in and to ancient Greece? The answers to all of these fundamental questions are not quite as straightforward as they may seem. Ancient Greece was never one single identifiable civilization or nation state in the way that, say, ancient Rome was; rather, ancient Greece was made up of a number of independent city-states and societies which existed more or less independently at different times. So we have, for example, the Minoan civilization on Crete, and, on the mainland or on islands nearby, Sparta, Mycenae, Athens, and Macedonia – all exerting power and influence, and often, if ever, only really coming together to do battle or forge alliances. Add to this the various Greek colonies scattered around the Mediterranean and the Black Sea and we have a very complex picture – geographically, politically, economically and socially. Ancient Greece was anything but homogenous; the ancient Greeks were never one people.

The aim of this short handbook is to simplify these complexities and provide an accessible history of the various facts, characters and events that make up the ancient Greeks and ancient Greece as we understand it today. To segment the extensive and complicated history of ancient Greece into 100 facts is no mean task. Concision, cohesion and comprehensiveness are the order of the day and questions as to what to leave out and what to include are nothing short of intractable. Indeed, this is a history of the ancient Greeks in 100 key facts and events – short, punchy pieces of historical information, which could form the nucleus of any history of ancient Greece, are delivered here in gobbets (as one of my Greek tutors used to call them), which can be ingested all in one go, or in meze-sized morsels. The choice is yours but, whichever way you approach this book, you will come away from it with a comprehensive history of the ancient Greeks and their various homelands, leaving you hungry to explore further the bits that particularly interest you.

Broadly speaking we can divide our history of ancient Greece into the following periods:

Minoan and early Helladic civilization in Crete between 3200 BC and 1200 BC.

The Bronze Age (2900–2000 BC), when early Aegean cultures start to emerge.

Mycenaean civilization in Greece, 1600–1100 BC; Mycenaeans control Crete 1500–1100 BC. Greeks take Troy.

Dark Ages from 1050 to 800 BC. Dorians and Aeolians destroy Mycenaean civilization.

The Archaic period (*c.* 800–*c.* 500 BC) comes to an end with the overthrow of the last tyrant of Athens and the birth of Athenian democracy in 508 BC. The Greek alphabet is formed from the Phoenician alphabet and western literature begins with Homer and Hesiod.

The Classical period (*c.* 500–323 BC): The destruction of Athens by the Persians, epitomized in the arts by the Parthenon. Politically, the period was dominated by Athens and the Delian League in the fifth century BC, but displaced by Sparta in the early fourth century BC. Power then shifted to Thebes and the Boeotian League and finally to the League of Corinth led by Macedon. This was the age of the Greco-Persian Wars and the rise of Macedon.

The Hellenistic period (323–146 BC) begins with the death of Alexander and saw Greek culture and power spread into the Near East. It ends with subjugation by the Romans at the Battle of Corinth in 146 BC.

1. THE EARLY ANCIENT GREEKS FOUGHT NO WARS

The ancient Greeks in their many guises did not just come from nowhere. It all started around 6500 BC when settlers arrived north of Thessaloniki via the Bosporus and the Danube – farmers spread south from Macedonia in search of more yielding, fruitful lands and Thessaly was cultivated at Sesklo. They brought pottery with them, formed without the aid of a wheel, and they built cabins of brick on stone foundations. Excavations from Nikomedeia have revealed plump fertility statuettes reminiscent of goddesses, while their lands on the alluvial plains seem to have been competently fertilized and farmed. As there was room for everyone, there was no need for war – this was the Golden Age referred to in later literature.

Crete enjoyed similar civilizing influences. From 5000 BC settlers came over from the Levant bringing with them livestock, usually living in caves in the warm and dry east; again, there was still no need for fortifications. From 4000 BC the Cyclades were settled. By 2750 hunters were, ominously, making copper daggers and spearheads and forming statuettes from the local marble. There were metalworkers, jewellers and stonecutters – specialists still unheard of in Crete and mainland Greece – and their villages began to resemble towns. Boats, signifying trade, began to appear on their pottery and the dead were buried in stone chamber tombs – the men with their weapons. They exported blades for farming to Crete and the mainland, and integrated there in the Early Helladic culture (3200/3100–2050/2001 BC).

By 2500 BC it seems they were trading in metals as far west as Spain, and nearer home their wares encouraged the development of a fortress at Hisarlik, or Troy. Trojan trade extended beyond the Troad to the Gallipoli peninsula, over to Lesbos and Lemnos and as far west as Macedonia.

From 2500 more immigrants from Asia Minor percolated into Crete and the Cyclades, some armed with bronze weapons; the Cycladic culture in turn influenced Tiryns and Mycenae. Around the same time we have evidence of a Thessalian settlement being razed. Clay phalli have also been unearthed, so the two together signify the new-found dominance of the male sex and their propensity for war. Villages were now being walled and copper axe-heads and gold jewellery have been found.

The Proto-Greeks probably arrived at the area now called Greece at the end of the third millennium BC. There were at least two migrations, the first being the Ionians and Aeolians, resulting in Mycenaean Greece by the sixteenth century BC, and the second, the Dorian invasion, around the eleventh century BC. Both migrations occur at critical periods: the Mycenaean at the transition to the Late Bronze Age and the Doric at the Bronze Age collapse. These Greeks of prehistory are seen in the Homeric epics as the ancestors of the Greeks of Homer's own time; the Mycenaean pantheon included many of the divinities such as Zeus, Poseidon and Hades who reappear in later Greek religion.

2. Knossos Was the Minoan's Principal City

Minoan civilization and culture is evident from around 2300 BC and, up until around 1950 BC, we can identify trade in faience, beads and ornaments from Egypt and ivory from Egypt or Syria. Vases are being made in marble and the olive plant joins grain as a staple. The large house excavated at Vasiliki would suggest an emerging class system. Copper is the metal of choice, in the absence of tin to make a viable alloy. Around 2000 Crete suddenly experienced an urban revolution: Knossos became the island's centre and principal city while other towns sprang up with streets lined with houses, dominated by a many-roomed multistorey palace. Roads were built from 1950 over the passes from Knossos and Phaistos complete with police posts, and the first attempts at a written language – Linear A. Bellicosity perhaps manifests itself in the shape of bronze, not least in the thrusting sword. There were still no fortifying city walls here, though the palaces have narrow entrances and a guardhouse to deter civil insurrection. Peace, however, still reigned between towns.

The lower orders were kept occupied with games, particularly highly hazardous bull-vaulting, as famously illustrated on frescoes – posh ladies are shown dancing or else sitting in a grandstand with their flounced skirts, puffed sleeves and breasts exposed. The men are ruddy and sunburnt; their women are white of complexion suggesting a life largely spent indoors out of the sun.

However, the peace was rudely interrupted between 1730 and 1570 by what may have been an earthquake or an invasion from Anatolia. The outcome, whatever the cause, was the destruction of the palaces at Knossos, Phaistos, Malia, and Kato Zakros. The island nevertheless was rebuilt with gusto. Trade flourished on the mainland with Mycenae, who in around 1420 repaid the Cretans by aggressively occupying the Minoan palace sites. The Mycenaeans adapted the Linear A Minoan script to meet the needs of their own language – a form of Greek written in Linear B.

Trade was vital and included saffron, ceramics, copper, and tin, and gold and silver. As well as Mycenae there were markets in Cyprus, Syria, Anatolia, Egypt, Mesopotamia and as far west as Spain. Minoan men wore loincloths and kilts. Women wore short-sleeved robes and layered, flounced skirts. The robes were open to the navel, leaving breasts exposed. Women also sometimes wore a strapless fitted bodice decorated with symmetrical geometric designs. Minoan religion focused on female deities, and Minoan women often officiated. Elsewhere the Cyclades waned while Thura thrived. Frescoes depicting swallows and lilies decorated rooms with furniture and painted pottery. Meanwhile, at Mylos the main town Phylakopi was fortified with huge walls.

'Minoan' derives from the mythical king Minos of Knossos; its first use is usually attributed to archaeologist Arthur Evans (1851–1941): Minos was associated with the labyrinth, which Evans identified at the site at Knossos.

3. The Greek Alphabet Was Derived from the Phoenician Alphabet

Before around 1950 BC, what we now call ancient Greek would not have been heard in what we now call ancient Greece. What was spoken would have been rooted in various Asia Minor languages, which later seem to have gone under the umbrella term 'Pelasgian', denoting aboriginal. Indeed most Greek place names owe nothing to Greek – for example, Knossos, Parnassus, Halicarnassus, Corinth and Athens. Words associated with plants, aspects of civilization and geographic names are similarly native and include, for example, cypress, narcissus, *plinthos* (brick), *thalassos* (sea) and most words for metals. The basic vocabulary, then, antedated Greek in many instances.

Greek, of course, is part of the Indo-European group of languages, along with Sanskrit, English, Latin and German. This would have been introduced into Greece through waves of migration – the Dorian invasions for example, from the north.

During the Mycenaean period (sixteenth century–twelfth century BC) , what is known as Linear B was used to render Greek language into written words, known also as Mycenaean Greek. This survived until the thirteenth century BC. By the ninth century a form of what we know as ancient Greek was more or less established, but, like all languages, it was dynamic, changing considerably over time in terms of grammar, pronunciation and vocabulary, with the added complication that it presented with many differing dialects, the chief of which were Attic and Ionic, Aeolic, Arcadocypriot, and Doric. Homeric Greek shows significant differences from Hellenistic (*koine*) Greek, used some 500 years later. In Homer's day, the Greek people were divided into three major divisions: Dorians,

Aeolians, and Ionians (including Athenians), each with their own recognisable and distinctive dialects.

The Greek alphabet was derived around the early eighth century from the earlier Phoenician alphabet, and was the first alphabetic script to offer distinct letters for vowels as well as consonants. It is the ancestor of the Latin and Cyrillic scripts.

Here is Herodotus' account (5, 58) written in the 450s BC: 'The Phoenicians who came with Cadmus ... introduced into Greece, after their settlement in the country, a number of accomplishments, of which the most important was writing, an art till then, I think, unknown to the Greeks. At first they used the same characters as all the other Phoenicians, but as time went on, and they changed their language, they also changed the shape of their letters. At that period most of the Greeks in the neighbourhood were Ionians; they were taught these letters by the Phoenicians and adopted them, with a few alterations, for their own use, continuing to refer to them as the Phoenician characters ...In the temple of Ismenian Apollo at Theba in Boeotia I have myself seen cauldrons with inscriptions cut on them in Cadmean characters—most of them not very different from the Ionian.'

Hyginus, (*Fabulae* 277ff) writing in the early Roman Empire, gives a less than historical account of the development of ancient Greek: 'The three Fates created the first five vowels of the alphabet and the letters B and T.'

4. THE THERA EARTHQUAKE WAS FELT AS FAR AWAY AS CHINA

Sometime around 1500 BC Mediterranean peace was well and truly shattered by the Minoan eruption of Thera (Santorini), one of the greatest volcanic events on the planet in recorded history. The eruption destroyed Thera, enveloping it in pumice, including the Minoan settlement at Akrotiri, as well as laying waste to communities and farmland on nearby islands and on the coast of Crete through a 40-ft tsunami four times greater than that which overwhelmed Karakatoa in 1883. On Thera, an evacuation saved most of the inhabitants, yet the explosion still killed up to 40,000 people in just a few hours, deposited volcanic ash across Asia, triggered a drop in global temperatures and created weird-coloured sunsets for three years. The blast was heard some 3,000 miles away. Its energy was tantamount to several hundred atomic bombs exploding simultaneously in a fraction of a second.

To what extent did the Thera cataclysm affect Minoan civilization? Some scholars argue that the ash layer and tsunami were of sufficient depth and magnitude to expedite the end of the Minoan civilization. The Minoans were a maritime power and depended on ships for their livelihood, so the Thera eruption would have had grave economic consequences – the drop in temperatures caused by massive amounts of sulphur dioxide spouted into the atmosphere led to several years of cold, wet summers with devastating effects on harvests. However, it seems likely that the Mycenaean invasion of Crete soon after may have happened anyway: the invaders were an advanced and aggressive military power with both an efficient navy and army. At best the eruption seriously disrupted Minoan society and commerce, making the

Minoans vulnerable to conquest by the Mycenaeans. At worst, it helped usher in a new age of belligerence.

The eruption was probably felt far beyond the Mediterranean. A volcanic winter from an eruption somewhere in the late seventeenth century BC has been attributed to Chinese records documenting the collapse of the Xia dynasty. The *Bamboo Annals* report that the collapse of the dynasty and the rise of the Shang dynasty, dated around 1618 BC, were characterised by 'yellow fog, a dim sun, then three suns, frost in July, famine, and the withering of all five cereals'. Nearer to home, heavy rainstorms, which wrecked much of Egypt and are described on the Tempest Stele of Ahmose I, have been attributed to short-term climatic changes caused by Thera.

Thera and its volcanic fallout may be at the roots of the myths of the Titanomachy in Hesiod's *Theogony*. Hesiod's description has been compared with volcanic activity, correlating Zeus's thunderbolts with volcanic lightning, the boiling earth and sea with a breach of the magma chamber, and Hesiodic flame and heat as with steam blast explosions. There is archaeological and volcanological evidence that Thera provided a basis for the myth of Atlantis, described by Plato in his *Timaeus* and *Critias*. There have even been attempts to establish a link between the eruption of Thera and the exodus of the Israelites from Egypt as described in the Bible.

5. Mycenaean Kings Were Tall, Bearded and Moustached

One of the Minoans' biggest trading partners was Mycenae, around 56 miles south-west of Athens and a mercantile success in her own right, due in part to her position on trading routes to the rest of Europe. At its peak around 1350 BC, it had a population of around 30,000. The prodigious wealth here is exemplified by the sumptuous grave burials, some of which were excavated by Heinrich Schliemann in the 1870s. The shaft graves yielded up ornaments of gold, silver and electrum, silver and bronze vases, bronze swords and daggers with gold and ivory handles, gold death masks, and jewellery – gold rings, buttons and bracelets. The *tour de force* was, of course, the electrum Mask of Agamemnon – evidence, according to Schliemann, of the historicity of Homer and Virgil. Some of the treasures bear the stamp of Cretan workmanship and provide evidence for the significant wealth enjoyed by the Mycenaeans and the Cretans in this period.

But the Mycenaeans were different. The kings at least were much taller, bearded and moustached in contrast to the clean-shaven Minoans; they had a liking for amber for their ornaments and they hunted on horse-drawn chariots – then unheard of on Crete. They depicted hunting and war scenes on the shaft graves and weapons.

Despite the commercial concord, the Cretans and the Mycenaeans were inevitable trade rivals. The former looked to Egypt, the Levant and Mycenae; the latter to the mainland and to Crete. Conflict was inevitable.

6. The Mycenaeans Cultivated a Patriarchal Religion

The Mycenaeans cultivated a patriarchal religion; their pantheistic pantheon comprised not only Minoan deities, but also a number of divinities who appear under different names with similar functions. Many of these names appear in the Linear B inscriptions but are also found later in classical Greece, for example Zeus, Hera, Poseidon, Athena, Hermes, and Dionysus. To the Mycenaeans any object possessed of an internal power (*anima*) was fair game for divinity; Mycenaean religion, apart from being polytheistic was syncretistic, with foreign deities swelling their pantheon. How far we can reliably differentiate between Minoan and Mycenaean religion, it is impossible to answer; however, we know that the Minoans had no truck with what later became the Olympian pantheon and that they focused more on the fertility function of Persephone, doomed to pass half the year in barren Hades, only enjoying rebirth for the other six months, to ensure the fecundity of the fields and crops. More focus on fertility is apparent through worship of the Great Mother, mother to Persephone.

The cult of the heroes was important to the Mycenaeans: great men of old who inhabited an island called Elysion, where they lived a happier afterlife. The less-exalted dead drifted aimlessly around the gloomy halls of Hades. The Mycenaeans probably believed in a future life if the two well-preserved bodies found in Shaft Grave VI are anything to go by, indicating that a form of embalming preceded the burial. In the shaft graves discovered by Schliemann, he discovered that the corpses were exposed to fire to preserve them.

7. King Minos Was Scalded to Death in His Bath

This is one of the great myths to come out of Crete. First King of Crete, son of Zeus and Europa, Minos is cursed with the gruesome task every nine years of making King Aegeus select seven young boys and seven young girls to be sent to Daedalus' labyrinth, to be devoured by the Minotaur. Homer dates him at around 1250 BC. On his mortal death he became, aptly, one of the judges of the dead in the underworld. Thucydides says that he formed the first navy – his palace, of course, was in Knossos. Zeus helped in formulating the Cretan constitution. Minos died a shocking death in Sicily where he had gone in hot pursuit of Daedalus, who had given Ariadne the clue that guided Theseus through the labyrinth and enabled him to kill the Minotaur – the offspring born from a bestial liaison between Minos' wife Pasiphae and a bull. Minos and his two brothers, Rhadamanthys and Sarpedon, were raised in the royal palace of Knossos. Minos married Pasiphae, daughter of the sun-god Helios. Their children included Phaedra, Ariadne, and Andregeos.

How did this happen? Minos was anxious to receive a sign from Poseidon that would endorse his accession as king. Poseidon duly sent a big white bull from the sea, which Minos was obliged to sacrifice to Poseidon. Minos, however, swapped it with a different bull. Poseidon was outraged and cursed Pasiphae with zoophilia. Daedalus constructed a wooden cow for her and she duly hid inside. The bull copulated with the wooden cow, impregnating Pasiphae, who eventually gave birth to the Minotaur – half man half bull – which was installed in the Labyrinth, built by Daedalus. To ensure no one would ever know about the Minotaur, or how to escape the Labyrinth (Daedalus was privy to both secrets), Minos imprisoned Daedalus and his son, Icarus, with the monster. Nevertheless, Daedalus and Icarus flew away on wings invented by Daedalus, but Icarus' wings melted because he famously flew too close to the sun. Icarus plummeted to the sea and drowned.

Minos was murdered by Daedalus in league with the daughter of Cocalus, king of Agrigentum, who poured boiling water over him while he was in the bath.

Another legend associated with King Minos is that of King Nisus of Megara, who, as a means to protect his city, kept a lock of red hair hidden in his own white hair. King Minos happened to besiege Megara, but Nisus knew that nothing could go wrong so long as the lock of red hair was still in place. However, Scylla, Nisus's daughter, fell in love with Minos, and as a token of her love for him, cut the lock of red hair from her father's head. Unfortunately, this killed Nisus, and consequently Megara fell. When Minos discovered that Scylla had been responsible for her father's death, he killed her. She was reincarnated as a seabird, to be pursued forever by her father Nisus, who had been turned into a sea eagle.

8. Michael Ventris Provided Evidence of a Greek-Speaking Minoan-Mycenaean Culture on Crete

The decipherment of Linear B was crucial to our understanding of the ancient Greek language. Linear B is a syllabic script used in writing Mycenaean Greek and predates the Greek alphabet by several centuries. Linear B comprises around eighty-seven syllabic signs and over 100 ideograms – signs which symbolize objects, units of measure or commodities. They are not pictures. As such, Linear B would seem to have been confined to business and administration usage. The thousands of clay tablets discovered in mainland Mycenae and Pylos and Knossos betray a relatively small number of different 'hands', suggesting that the script was used exclusively by a guild of professional scribes in the central palaces from around 1200 BC. It was deciphered between AD 1951 and 1953 by English architect and self-taught linguist Michael Ventris. His discovery was significant because it provided evidence of a Greek-speaking Minoan-Mycenaean culture on Crete, and showed Greek writing some 600 years earlier than what was thought existed at the time.

The 6,058 known inscriptions have been found on tablets, vases and other vessels. It would seem that cities and palaces used Linear B for records of the distribution of goods – wool, sheep, and grain being the most popular commodities. At Knossos, impressions left in the clay from the weaving of the baskets would suggest that the tablets were kept in baskets on shelves. The buildings they were in were destroyed by fires, and many of the tablets were hard-baked.

9. The Gods Started the Trojan War

1183 BC is the favoured date for the legendary fall of Troy at the hands of the Mycenaean Greek (Achaean) armies under the command of Agamemnon and the deployment of the famous, duplicitous Trojan horse. This was ten years after the start of the war on a Troy (VIIa) that excavations have revealed was full of bins and pits dug for storage – storage of grain and other staples dragged in by country folk seeking refuge and making preparations for a long siege. The numerous shanties were the other defining characteristic.

The gods started it when Athena, Hera, and Aphrodite squabbled after Eris, the goddess of all things disputatious and discordant, mischievously gave them a golden apple, the Apple of Discord, inscribed 'for the fairest'. Eris had been denied access to the wedding of Peleus and Thetis and was somewhat insulted as a result. Zeus had had enough: he sent the three quarrelling goddesses to Trojan Paris for judging. Paris, ignorant of who he really was, was working as a shepherd in a bid to thwart a prophecy that would see him cause the end of Troy. After bathing in the spring of Ida, the three goddesses appeared before him naked, either in an erotic bid to help them win, or at Paris' bidding. Paris could not decide between them, so the goddesses resorted to more bribery: Athena offered Paris wisdom, skill in battle, and the ability to compete with the greatest warriors; Hera offered him political power and control over all of Asia; and Aphrodite offered him the love of the most beautiful woman in the world, Helen of Sparta. Paris gave the apple to Aphrodite, and eventually returned to Troy with her.

Agamemnon, king of Mycenae and the brother of Helen's husband Menelaus, led an expedition of Achaean (Greek) troops to Troy and besieged the city for ten years to avenge Paris' impudence. Heroes fell, including Greek Achilles and Ajax, and the Trojans Hector and Paris, before Troy itself fell. The Greeks massacred the Trojans, sparing a few women and children who were enslaved, but made the mistake of hubristically desecrating the Trojans temples and incurring the wrath of the gods. As result, few of the Greeks reached home safely.

The siege is, of course, described in Homer's epic *Iliad*, with aspects appearing in the fragmentary *Epic Cycle*, in Greek and Roman tragedy and in the work of Virgil and Ovid. The most famous spin-offs are the *Odyssey* – the long journey home to Ithaca of Odysseus – and the equally circuitous and eventful journey made by Trojan Aeneas to Italy to found the city and empire that was Rome, and to establish the Roman race as narrated in Virgil's *Aeneid*. The Trojan horse and Aeneas' flight from the burning ruin that was Troy is described in vivid detail in Book 2 of the *Aeneid*.

10. THE TOP GODS FORMED AN ELITE GROUP KNOWN AS THE TWELVE OLYMPIANS

We have already noted that Greek religion was polytheistic and syncretic; the pantheon was, for the most part, anthropomorphic – there were a few half men-half animals and the odd occasional metamorphosis. It was also very hierarchical, with the most important Olympians forming an elite group known as the Twelve Olympians, or the Dodekatheon (Greek: Δωδεκάθεον). The Olympians got to where they were in a war of the gods in which Zeus led his siblings to victory over the Titans. The twelve who qualified for this supreme position are usually Zeus, Hera, Poseidon, Demeter, Athena, Apollo, Artemis, Ares, Aphrodite, Hephaestus, Hermes and either Hestia or Dionysus. Hades, or Pluto, was not always included because his realm was the underworld and he could never make it up to Olympus.

Zeus King of the gods and ruler of Mount Olympus; god of the sky, lightning, thunder, law, order, justice. Youngest child of the Titans Cronus and Rhea.

Hera Queen of the gods and the goddess of marriage and family. Wife and sister of Zeus.

Poseidon God of the seas, earthquakes, and tsunami. Brother of Zeus and Hades.

Demeter Goddess of fertility, agriculture, nature, and the seasons. Middle daughter of Cronus and Rhea.

Athena Goddess of wisdom, reason, literature, handicrafts and science, defense and strategic warfare. Daughter of Zeus and the Oceanid Metis, she rose from her father's head fully grown and in full battle armour after he swallowed her mother.

Apollon God of light, prophecy, inspiration, poetry, music and arts, medicine and healing. Son of Zeus and Leto.

Artemis Goddess of the hunt, virginity, archery, the moon, and all animals. Daughter of Zeus and Leto and twin sister of Apollo.

Ares God of war, violence, and bloodshed. Symbols include the boar, serpent, dog, vulture, spear, and shield. Son of Zeus and Hera, all the other gods (except Aphrodite) hated him.

Aphrodite Goddess of love, beauty and sex. Daughter of Zeus and the Oceanid Dione, or born from the sea foam after Uranus' semen dripped into the sea after he was castrated by his youngest son, Cronus, who then threw his father's genitals into the sea. Aphrodite was married to Hephaestus, and her name gives us the word 'aphrodisiac'.

Hephaestus Blacksmith and craftsman of the gods; god of fire and the forge. Son of Hera. Married to Aphrodite.

Hermes Messenger of the gods; god of commerce, thieves, eloquence and streets. Son of Zeus and the nymph Maia.

Hestia Vesta Goddess of the hearth and of domesticity and the family. She is the first child of Cronus and Rhea, eldest sister of Hades, Demeter, Poseidon, Hera, and Zeus.

Dionysus God of wine, salubrious behaviour and drunken orgies. Patron god of theatre. Son of Zeus and the mortal Theban princess Semele. Married to the Cretan princess Ariadne. The youngest Olympian god, and the only one to have a mortal mother.

All human life is there...

11. Homer Places Doctors on a Social Standing Equal to Seers, Shipwrights and Musicians

Modern medicine owes much to ancient Greek medicine. The Hippocratics and Hippocrates were particularly cutting-edge and have been enduringly influential. In the Roman Empire Galen was a prolific writer on all aspects of medicine. Soranus was a noted gynaecologist.

The earliest known Greek medical school opened its doors in Cnidus in 700 BC. Alcmaeon, author of the first anatomy text and atlas, worked at this school, where the practice of observing patients was established. The Greeks imported Egyptian potions and medicines into their own pharmacopoeia. The most famous and influential medical school was the school of Greek medicine in Alexandria – important because human dissection could be performed here but not in Greece or Rome.

Homer, in the *Odyssey* (17, 382-384), places doctors on a social standing equal to seers, shipwrights and musicians – useful and valuable, in other words; in the *Iliad* (11, 514-515) he values military surgeons highly. His depiction of the terrible trauma suffered by Erymas with his brain cleaved, his teeth knocked out, with blood spurting from his eyeballs, nose and mouth is typical of the vivid descriptions in the *Iliad* of battlefield injuries.

The *Hippocratic Corpus* collects a number of medical treatises dating mainly from the fifth and fourth centuries BC. The sixty or so texts are written by up to twenty authors; they comprise textbooks, lectures, notes, research papers and numerous case histories, many of which conclude with the death of the patient. The content is aimed both at the specialist and the layman. The *Hippocratic Oath* – a key tenet of which is 'help, or at least do no harm' – endures today as a cornerstone of ethical medical practice. Aristotle (384–322 BC) expatiated on human medical matters in his *History of Animals* and *Generation of Animals*.

Both Diocles of Carystus and Cleophantus wrote a *Gynaecology*. Fourth-century Diocles coined the term 'anatomy' and was also celebrated for his work on diet and nutrition, as well as for a book on comparative anatomy. Cleophantus' brother, Erasistratus (born *c*. 304 BC), is noted for his work on anatomy, cardiac physiology, and, particularly, the vascular system. Herophilos (335–280) produced nine medical books (all lost) including a *Maiotikon* – a midwifery text. He pioneered human dissection and founded the medical school in Alexandria.

A medical practitioner in Greece was viewed no differently from any other craftsman; he would learn his trade by attaching himself to an experienced practitioner, for a fee, having spent time in one or other of the medical schools. As a pupil he, or she, would help attend to the patient and assist in operations. On completion of the training the novice doctor would practice as a peripatetic to gain experience, and after this the best trainees would be hired by the state.

The surgeon was very much a generalist with a list that would have taken in fractures and dislocations, trepanning of the skull, cataract operations, maxillofacial surgery, ENT procedures, lithotomy, and obstetrics and gynaecology.

12. The *Polis* Was the Defining Political and Social Unit

We have already noted that ancient Greece was never a homogenous country or state in the way that ancient Rome was. The *polis* was the defining political and social unit. Ancient Greece was essentially a conglomeration of individual independent states with political autonomy, their own local government, cults and festivals, judicial system, social institutions, armies and navies and foreign and domestic policy. Border disputes and conflict were common. They each went their own way in trade, political alliances and wars; they each had their own currencies and coinage, which reinforced their individuality (for, example, Athenian coins often depicted the city's symbol, the owl); some *poleis* such as Corinth developed distinctive, identifiable pottery.

There were, nevertheless, common features: they usually had a city centre (*agora*) for civic and commercial activity and entertainment often fortified with a wall and with a sacred centre built on a natural acropolis or harbour, which controlled the surrounding territory (*chora*). Many *poleis* also had a special space either for political assemblies or entertainment in the shape of a theatre and gymnasium.

The *polis* grew out of the Dark Ages that followed the fall of the Mycenaean civilization. By the eighth century BC this urbanisation was in full swing, leading eventually to over 1,000 *poleis*, the most important of which were Athens, Sparta, Corinth, Thebes, Syracuse, Aegina, Rhodes, Argos, Eretria, and Elis. The biggest were Athens and Sparta, although with some 8,500 km² Sparta was exceptional – most *poleis* were much smaller. However, *poleis* such as Athens, Rhodes and Syracuse could expand their territory and influence through navies, which allowed them to colonise and control expansive areas of territory across the Aegean as mother cities – the metropolis. Magna Graecia (southern Italy and Sicily mainly), the Black Sea shores and Ionia, for example, were major areas of colonisation.

One of the principles of the *polis* was that, theoretically at least, all male citizens enjoyed equal political rights based on ownership of property. In practice, whatever the prevailing political system – tyranny, oligarchy or democracy – political power was in the hands of a few aristocratic families who monopolised all the important positions in the *polis,* such as membership of warrior assemblies, magistracies and the higher military ranks. Women were excluded from public life.

It was not total independence though: wars against foreign enemies brought *poleis* together (for example, the fifth-century Persian wars), and leagues were formed to produce strength in numbers (for example, the Delian and Achaean leagues). Festivals too forged links where *poleis* competed against each other, the most famous being the Olympic Games.

In Athens after the reign of King Kodros, the hereditary monarchy was replaced around 1080 BC with life *archontes*, selected from the aristocracy – nine of whom were being appointed annually by the sixth century. The office of king (*basileus*) still looked after religious affairs while the *polemarchos* was in charge of military matters. Later, one single *archon* took precedence as the eponymous archon, after whom the year was named.

13. THE *ILIAD* IS ONE OF THE OLDEST SURVIVING WORKS OF WESTERN LITERATURE

The *Iliad*, along with its sister epic poem, the *Odyssey*, is one of the oldest surviving works of western literature, written around 750 BC by a poet called Homer. It describes the final days of the ten-year-long siege of Troy by a confederation of Greek armies but, with numerous flashbacks, gives a vivid picture more or less of the entire war. It runs to over 15,600 lines in twenty-four books.

The war was triggered when Aphrodite bribed Paris with Helen, the world's most beautiful woman, in order to get her clutches on the coveted Apple of Discord. Paris needed no persuading to elope with her. We begin in the middle, *in medias res,* near the end of the Trojan War. Chryses, a Trojan priest, offers to buy back his daughter Chryseis from Agamemnon; Agamemnon refuses. Chryses prays to Apollo for help; Apollo delivers a plague on the Greek army.

Achilles convenes a meeting to resolve the issue of the plague. Agamemnon agrees to return Chryseis, but takes Achilles's girl, Briseis, as compensation. Achilles sulks in his tent, withdraws his support for Agamemnon and prepares to go home. Odysseus takes Chryseis to her father. Apollo ends the plague.

Achilles asks his mother, Thetis, to ask Zeus to bring the Greeks to the brink so that Agamemnon will realise how much he needs him. Zeus agrees and sends a dream to Agamemnon, urging him to attack the city. Homer describes each of the Greek armies, and then the Trojan armies.

Paris offers to bring an end to the war by fighting a duel with Menelaus. Paris is beaten, but Aphrodite rescues him and leads him to bed with Helen before Menelaus could kill him. Zeus has Trojan Pandaros break the truce by wounding Menelaus with an arrow. Agamemnon rouses the Greeks and battle commences.

Diomedes wounds Aphrodite while heroes fight gods. Hector rallies the Trojans and stops a rout. Hector fights an inconclusive duel with Ajax. Agamemnon now sees his error and sends a delegation to offer Briseis and gifts to Achilles. An angry Achilles rejects Agamemnon's offer.

Odysseus and Diomedes launch a guerrilla raid on the Trojan lines, killing the Trojan Dolon. The Trojans attack the Greek wall and overwhelm the Greeks; Hector charges in. Achilles relents, and lends Patroclus his armour; Patroclus kills the Trojan hero Sarpedon. Patroclus, ignoring Achilles's orders, reaches the gates of Troy and is killed by Hector.

Achilles vows to take vengeance on Hector. In the morning, Achilles drives his chariot into battle. Hector resolves to confront Achilles. Achilles stabs Hector in the neck. Before dying, Hector reminds Achilles that he is fated to die in the war as well. Achilles takes Hector's body.

Unhappy at Achilles's abuse of Hector's corpse, Zeus decides that it must be returned to Priam, who takes a wagon out of Troy and enters the Greek camp. He implores Achilles to let him have his son's body. Achilles is moved to tears. Priam carries Hector's body back into Troy. Hector is buried, and the city mourns.

14. The *Odyssey*: a Tale of Horizontal Collaboration and Other Trials

A sequel of sorts to the *Iliad*, the *Odyssey* is around 12,000 lines long, in twenty-four books. It tells the exhilarating story of Trojan warrior Odysseus' highly eventful journey home from Troy to Ithaca and the trials and tribulations he faces over his ten-year-long odyssey.

The first four books are concerned with Odysseus' patient wife, Penelope, and his son, Telemachus, and the problems they face with Penelope's insistent suitors.

Antinous and Eurymachus are the main problems and go so far as to plot to assassinate Telemachus. Telemachus visits Sparta where King Menelaus reveals that Odysseus is alive but held captive by the nymph Calypso. The gods decide to free Odysseus from Calypso after seven years' detention and horizontal collaboration.

Poseidon, god of the sea, is angry because Odysseus has put the Cyclops' one and only eye out, so he shipwrecks Odysseus on Phaeacia, ruled by King Alcinous.

A terrible storm, brought on by Athena, then blows them to the land of the Lotus-eaters. Their lotus plant robs Odysseus and his men of memory and motivation, and Odysseus has to drag his men away and resume the journey.

As we have seen, Odysseus is then attracted to the land of the Cyclops – barbaric, cannibalistic, one-eyed giants. One of them, Polyphemus, traps Odysseus and some of his men in his cave. To escape, Odysseus blinds him, thus incurring the wrath of the giant's father, Poseidon.

Aeolus, god of the winds, is a helpful ally and captures all the bad winds in a bag for Odysseus, who sails within sight of Ithaca. Unfortunately, his men open the bag and the escaping winds blow them back to an annoyed Aeolus.

The cannibalistic Laestrygonians then sink all the ships but Odysseus'; the survivors reach Aeaea, home of the witchy woman Circe, who turns the crew into pigs. With advice and an antidote from Hermes, Odysseus becomes her lover. She tells Odysseus that he must sail to the Land of the Dead, where he reviews a parade of Greek heroes and his mother, as well as receiving a prophecy from the blind seer Tiresias. Odysseus resumes his journey.

They survive the Sirens' seductive songs and an attack by Scylla, to arrive next at the island of the sun god Helios. Despite advice to the contrary, his men feast on the cattle of the sun god. Zeus is outraged and destroys the ship as the Greeks depart, killing all of them except Odysseus, who, now alone, is washed ashore on Calypso's island, where he tarries for those seven years .

Odysseus returns home disguised as a beggar. Eurycleia, a nurse who looked after Odysseus when he was a child, recognises Odysseus from an old scar. Penelope arranges a contest, vowing to wed any man who can string the bow of Odysseus and shoot an arrow through a dozen axes as he used to do. The suitors all fail; Odysseus, of course, succeeds and he and Telemachus slaughter the suitors. Odysseus and Penelope are reunited.

15. There Was No Homer

Who was Homer? Homer is thought to have lived in the eighth century BC, some 170 years after the events he describes in the *Iliad*. We can begin to get a picture of how important Homer was considered in the classical Greek world from Plato: in the *Republic* he describes him as *protos didaskalos*, first teacher, of the tragedians, the *hegemon paideias*, leader of Greek culture, and the *ten Hellada pepaideukon*, teacher of [all] Greece. Interestingly, Homer's output is around 50 per cent speeches: these have provided models in rhetoric and speech-making and have been emulated throughout the ancient world. To illustrate how ubiquitous Homer's work was and how frequently he was quoted or referenced, Homeric fragments account for nearly half of all Greek literary papyrus finds in Egypt.

Controversy, however, continues to rage over whether Homer actually existed at all, as a single real, identifiable poet. Martin West argues that 'Homer' is 'not the name of a historical poet, but a fictitious or constructed name'. Oliver Taplin would have it that the accounts of a Homeric life "are largely…" demonstrable fictions' and that Homer is 'a historical context for the poems'. G. S. Kirk said that, 'Antiquity knew nothing definite about the life and personality of Homer.' Nineteen different places claim Homer as their son, including Athens; Chios and Smyrna, however, seem to have the best claim.

In the sixth and fifth centuries many more works other than just the *Iliad* and *Odyssey* were attributed to Homer. They included the whole of the *Epic Cycle*, which took in poems about the Trojan War, such as the *Little Iliad*, the *Nostoi*, the *Cypria, Aethiopia, Iliu Persis* (Sack of Troy), *Telegony* and the *Epigoni*, as well as the Theban poems about Oedipus and his sons. The corpus of *Homeric*

Hymns, the comic mini-epic *Batrachomyomachia, The Frog-Mouse War*, and the *Margites*, were also attributed to him along with the *Capture of Oechalia* and the *Phocais*. The *Epic Cycle (Epikos Kuklos)* was a collection of ten epic poems penned by different authors, which are stories covering Greek mythology. All, like the *Iliad* and *Odyssey*, are composed in hexameters.

Typically, Homer is depicted as a blind, bearded man; his famous poetry is an enduring legacy of an oral tradition which saw centuries of singer-poets, bards, handing down from one generation to the next, exciting stories and legends of the past. Before Homer, oral composition was the order of the day: it may well be that Homer came just at the right time to take advantage of the newly available Greek writing alphabet and the services, perhaps, of scribes.

The *Iliad* and the *Odyssey* crop up throughout modern literature: the *Odyssey* can be seen in James Joyce's *Ulysses*, while the tale of Achilles in the *Iliad* has echoes in J. R. R. Tolkien's *The Fall of Gondolin*. The Coen Brothers' film *O Brother, Where Art Thou?* owes something to the *Odyssey*.

16. HESIOD HAS MADE SIGNIFICANT CONTRIBUTIONS TO THE LITERATURE ON FARMING, ECONOMIC THOUGHT, ASTRONOMY AND ANCIENT TIME-KEEPING

The contribution of Hesiod to Greek literature and mythology is enormous; however, he has forever languished in the long shadow of Homer and is often somewhat overlooked. Hesiod has made significant contributions to the writings of farming, economic thought, astronomy and ancient time-keeping. He is thought to have flourished between 700 and 650 BC. His complete surviving works are *Works and Days*, *Theogony*, and the attributed *Shield of Heracles*.

The *Theogony* deals with the origins of the world, cosmogony, and of the gods, theogony, beginning with Chaos, Gaia, Tartarus and Eros, and their genealogy. It explains for us how Zeus attained supreme power: the castration of Uranus by Cronus and the expulsion of Cronus and the Titans – the former gods – by the Olympians. According to Herodotus, Hesiod's version became the established version for all Greeks. Hesiod includes the un-Homeric chthonic Hecate, a description of Tartarus and the myth of Prometheus.

The *Works and Days* is over 800 lines long, and is based on two universal truths: work is the universal lot of man and the man who is prepared to work will succeed. It represents one of the earliest known disquisitions on economic thought. Hesiod lays out the Five Ages of Man, prescribing a life of honest hard work and vilifying dishonesty and idleness; labour is the source of all good in the world. It includes the famous myth of Pandora, and seafaring and religious and social conduct are also covered. The work ends with a calendar of days recommended for various horticultural and agricultural activity, and an *Ornithomanteia* – bird omens.

The *Shield of Heracles* is a Greek epic poem that was attributed to Hesiod during antiquity. Its subject is the expedition of Heracles and Iolaus against Cycnus, the son of Ares, who challenged Heracles to combat while Heracles was passing through Thessaly. It influenced Virgil's Shield of Aeneas (*Aeneid* viii.617-731) and Crenaeus' shield in Statius' *Thebaid* (ix.332-338).

Other works attributed to Hesiod included the *Catalogue of Women* or *Ehoiai*, a mythological roll call of mortal women who had mated with gods, and of their offspring; the *Megalai Ehoiai*, a poem similar to the *Catalogue of Women*; *Wedding of Ceyx*, Heracles' attendance at the wedding of Ceyx; *Melampodia*, a genealogical poem which deals with the families of, and myths associated with, the great mythical seers of mythology; *Idaean Dactyls*, a work about mythological smelters, the Idaean Dactyls; *Descent of Perithous*, the *katabasis* of Theseus and Perithous to Hades; *Precepts of Chiron*, a didactic work revealing the teachings of Chiron to Achilles; *Megala Erga* or *Great Works*, a poem similar to the *Works and Days; Astronomia*, an astronomical poem; *Aegimius*, a heroic epic; *Kiln or Potters*, a poem asking Athena to provide assistance to potters; *a Dirge for Batrachus*, the love of Hesiod's life.

17. OUR WORD 'PANIC' COMES FROM THE GOD PAN

There were other gods and goddesses installed on Olympus other than the superior Twelve Olympians:

Hades God of the Underworld, the dead and everything under the Earth. He was born into the first Olympian generation, the elder brother of Zeus, Poseidon, Hera, and Demeter, and younger brother of Hestia.

Heracles A divine hero, the son of Zeus and Alcmene. The greatest of all Greek heroes, a paragon of masculinity and a champion against chthonic monsters.

Persephone Queen of the Underworld and a daughter of Demeter and Zeus; goddess of spring time. She was the consort of Hades. Demeter was driven out of her mind by this and neglected her duty to the earth, so that nothing grew. Zeus ordered Hades to allow Persephone to leave the Underworld and go back to her mother. Hades complied, but because Persephone had eaten six of the twelve pomegranate seeds in the Underworld, she had to spend six months in the Underworld each year. This created the seasons: for six months everything flourished, then for the rest of the year everything died.

Asclepius The god of medicine and healing.

Eros The god of sexual love and beauty.

Hebe The daughter of Zeus and Hera and the cup-bearer for the deities on Mount Olympus, serving their nectar and ambrosia, until she was married to Heracles.

Pan The god of nature, shepherds and flocks, mountains, hunting, the forest, and country music. Our word 'panic' comes from Pan and the great war cry that instilled fear and panic into all his enemies.

18. More than Thirty Greek City-States had Colonies around the Mediterranean

'Greek' here presents something of a misnomer, since the age of expansion between 734 and 580 BC was spearheaded, not by a concerted Greek action over time, but by individual *poleis* acting with political and commercial autonomy. The *poleis* were keen to acquire more land, to foster trade and to stamp their influence at a distance from the mother city, the metropolis.

Al Mina on the coast of Syria and Pithekoussai at Ischia in the Bay of Naples were the first, established by Euboea between 900 and 800 BC. Chalcis and Eretria were the pioneers. In all, more than thirty Greek city-states had colonies around the Mediterranean. Miletus was the most active with ninety or so colonies stretching the length of the Mediterranean, the Black Sea and Anatolia in the east, including Kyzikos (founded 675 BC), Sinope (*c*. 631 BC), Pantikapaion (*c*. 600 BC), and Olbia (*c*. 550 BC) to the southern coast of the Iberian Peninsula in the west, as well as several colonies on the Libyan coast. Eventually, most of the Black Sea coast was populated by Greek colonies from one *polis* or another. Megara was another active mother city and founded Chalcedon (*c*. 685 BC), Byzantium (668 BC), and Herakleia Pontike (560 BC). Competition came mainly in the form of the Phoenicians, who were very active in the Levant, North Africa and southern Spain.

There were numerous settlements along the Aegean coast of Ionia (Asia Minor) from the eighth century BC, including Miletos, Ephesos, Smyrna, and Halikarnassos, with Athens at the forefront of colonisation. Greek culture and learning thrived, particularly in science, mathematics, and philosophy, palmed column capitals, sphinxes, and 'orientalising' pottery designs. In southern Italy and Sicily the Greek influence was so great they called the region 'Greater Greece' (*Megalē Hellas* or *Magna Graecia*). Some of the premier colonies in Italy were Cumae (the first Italian colony, founded *c.* 740 BC by Chalcis), Naxos (734 BC, Chalcis), Sybaris (*c.* 720 BC, Achaean/Troezen), Croton (*c.* 710 BC, Achaean), Tarentum (706 BC, Sparta), Rhegium (*c.* 720 BC, Chalcis), Elea (*c.* 540 BC, Phocaea), Thurri (*c.* 443 BC, Athens), and Heraclea (433 BC, Tarentum). On Sicily the main colonies included Syracuse (733 BC, founded by Corinth), Gela (688 BC, Rhodes and Crete), Selinous (c. 630 BC), Himera (*c.* 630 BC, Messana), and Akragas (*c.* 580 BCE, Gela). Further afield, Massalia (Phocaea) was a key colony in southern France.

There were two types of colony: an *apoikia* (ἀποικία) – a city-state in its own right; and an *emporion* (ἐμπορίον) – a Greek trading colony. So ubiquitous were Greek colonies that in the first century BC, Cicero, in the *De Republica*, said 'It were as though a Greek fringe has been woven about the shores of the barbarians.'

19. Greek Magic First Appears in Homer's *Odyssey* Where Odysseus Meets the Sexy Circe

How did magic manifest itself in Greece? What do Greek myth and legend tell of the meddling magic men and women? How did they meddle and dabble, and to what end? Since our knowledge of Greek magic comes mainly through Greek literature, we now take a magical tour with Greek writers through the centuries.

We first encounter Greek magic in Homer's *Odyssey*. Here Odysseus meets the sexy, and witchy, Circe, who wields a staff (*rabdos*) and concocts a potion, which changes Odysseus' crew into pigs. (We discuss Circe in detail in fact 55.)

Other magical episodes in Homer include necromancy, the sorcerous *molu* compound that Mercury prescribes to Odysseus to protect him against Circe's spells. Athena later transforms Odysseus into a beggar with her *rabdos*, and the thieving Autolycus sings a spell as an unconventional treatment for the hero's wound from a savage boar. Proteus predicts Menelaus' destiny in Elysium, witchy Circe instructs Odysseus to visit the Underworld as referred to above, Calypso detains Odysseus with a Siren-like song, and Odysseus buries his comrades at sea. A spell is used to staunch the blood from a wound sustained by Odysseus after a fight with a wild boar.

Helen of Troy prescribes a beneficent, recreational *pharmakon* to the soldiers of her husband Menelaus. The twin gates of dreams are described, and in the last book of the *Odyssey* Homer describes the spirits of Achilles and Agamemnon in Hades. In the *Iliad* Homer describes the ghost of Achilles' comrade Patroclus and tells the story of how Hera, queen of the gods, acquires Aphrodite's love amulet in order to seduce Zeus, her unfaithful husband. These passages establish how magic and witchcraft worked in the late Greek Bronze Age, the Homeric era of around the thirteenth century BC. Over hundreds of years, audiences listened to these stories of magic and the occult, no doubt associating them with similar experiences in their own times and communities.

Hesiod described the hellish world of Tartarus and its inhabitants in some detail. He also gives us a biography of Hecate, the witch goddess. Medea (the daughter of Hecate) is seen by many as the archetypal witch, and therefore is omnipresent in ancient literature on the supernatural.

The poet Pindar adds to our knowledge of the supernatural in Greece by telling how the dead were led to the kingdom of Hades and judged there. Another two fragments of his poems describe the paradise-like land of Elysium and the transmigration of souls (basically, reincarnation). Pindar also cannot resist including Medea in a scene in which Aphrodite, paradoxically, uses magic to help Jason win Medea's heart.

Pindar also describes the skills of Asclepius, god of medicine, and shows how blurred the line was between 'conventional' and magical medicine. Incantations are used alongside drugs. *Pharmaka* are useful herbs or magical potions, and both were imbibed and used in amulets.

20. Athens Started to Exert Itself in 632 BC When the Athenians Resisted the Tyranny of Cylon

Politically, Athens, in Attica, started to exert itself in 632 BC when the Athenians resisted the tyranny of Cylon. Athens succeeded in bringing other towns of Attica under its rule, and this *synoikismos* created the largest and wealthiest state on the Greek mainland, but a by-product was the creation a larger class of people excluded from political life by the aristocrats.

Social unrest was everywhere, so the Areopagus appointed Draco to draft a strict new code of law (hence our word 'draconian') to restore some kind of order. Execution was the punishment for most transgressions. When Draco's laws failed, they appointed Solon, with a mandate to form a new, more moderate, constitution in 594 BC. This laid the groundwork for democracy in Athens. It was followed by the largely benign tyranny of Peistratus and Hippias, his son, which lasted up to 510. All went well until Hippias' younger brother, Hipparkhos, was assassinated in a love affair gone wrong in 514 BC. Hippias inflicted a reign of terror, which culminated in the overthrow of the Peisistratid tyranny in the Athenian Revolt of 510 BC – supported by Sparta led by Kleomenes. In the aftermath of the coup, and after settling affairs with Spartan factions such as Isagoras, Cleisthenes was appointed to reform the government and the legislature.

The first real signs of democracy emerged in 508 under Cleisthenes while Athens incurred the wrath of Persia through its support of the Ionian Revolt. In 499 BC Athens posted troops to assist the Ionian Greeks of Asia Minor, who were rising up against the Persian Empire. This sparked two Persian invasions of Greece: in 490 BC the Athenians, led by Miltiades, defeated the first Persian invasion under Darius I at the Battle of Marathon. Ten years later the Persians were back under Darius's son, Xerxes. A small Greek force holding the pass of Thermopylae was defeated. The Athenians evacuated Athens, which fell to the Persians. Later, the Athenians, led by Themistocles, engaged the superior Persian navy in the Battle of Salamis. This was when Xerxes, with supreme arrogance, built a throne on the beach from which to watch the Greek navy being defeated, but instead, his Persians were routed. In 479 BC, the Athenians and Spartans, with their allies, defeated the Persian army at the Battle of Plataea.

Athens came out of this as the supreme naval power in Greece. They formed the Delian League, to create a cohesive Greek network among city-states and defend against further Persian assaults. Under the leadership of Pericles, it became so powerful that the Athenian Empire could effectively dictate the laws, customs, and trade policy of all her neighbours in Attica and the Aegean islands.

By the 460s the emergent democracy had finally shrugged off many of its aristocratic vestiges. Athens entered the First Peloponnesian War of 461–446.

21. By 650 BC Sparta had Become the Dominant Military Land-Power in Ancient Greece

Sparta was another of Greece's leading city-states. It emerged as a political force and entity around the tenth century BC when invading Dorians subjugated the local population. By 650 BC it had become the dominant military land-power in ancient Greece. Due largely to its military prowess, Sparta was the overall leader of the combined Greek forces during the Graeco-Persian Wars.

Many aspects of Spartan society and their political system set it apart from other *poleis*; uniquely, life there was focused on military training and excellence. Spartans were classified as Spartiates (Spartan citizens, who enjoyed full rights), *mothakes* (non-Spartan freemen raised as Spartans), *perioiko*i (freedmen), and helots (state-owned serfs, enslaved non-Spartan local population). It was the Spartiates who underwent the rigorous *agoge* training and education regimen; Spartan military phalanges were among the best in battle.

Spartan women enjoyed considerably more rights, freedom and equality than women elsewhere in the ancient world. Plutarch's *Moralia* includes a collection of 'Sayings of Spartan Women', including one attributed to Gorgo, the wife of Leonidas I. When asked by a woman from Attica why Spartan women were the only women in the world who could dominate men, she replied, 'Because we are the only women who are mothers of men'.

Spartan citizens did not concern themselves with farming; the helots did all that – they were permitted to keep a percentage of the produce they cultivated, and they were also regularly purged to keep them firmly in their place. They could also be conscripted into the army.

Things Spartan held a fascination all of their own: Laconophilia or Laconism is a term meaning love or admiration of Sparta and of the Spartan culture or constitution. The term derives from Laconia, the region of the Peloponnese where Sparta was. Admirers typically praise their bravery and success in war, their 'laconic' austerity and self-restraint, the stability of their political life, and their constitution, with its tripartite mixed government. A new verb was even coined – λακωνίζειν, which means to act like a Laconian. Some Athenians thought that the Spartan constitution was better than their own and went so far as to imitate Spartan manners by sporting long hair and going unwashed, as the Spartiates did. Platonists often saw Sparta as the ideal state: strong, brave, and devoid of commercial corruption.

On the other hand, Herodotus paints a picture of Spartans as backward, hesitant, difficult, corrupt and naïve. In his *Politics*, Aristotle sees the Spartans as rebellious – their women over luxurious, their magistrates irresponsible, and they evade taxes – so the city is impoverished and the citizens are greedy. In short, they are incompetent and fraudulent.

In 480 BC a small force of 300 Spartans, Thespians (700), and Thebans (400) led by King Leonidas made their legendary last stand at the Battle of Thermopylae against the Persian army on whom they visited substantial casualties before being encircled. The superior weaponry, strategies and tactics, and bronze armour of the Greek hoplites and their phalanx, proved their worth in 479 when Sparta led a Greek alliance against the Persians at the Battle of Plataea.

22. Sparta Had a Very Well-Oiled War Machine

Sparta was an out-and-out military society. Lycurgus, in the eighth century BC, summed it up when he said that Sparta's walls were built of men, not bricks. Sparta was a well-oiled war machine that always needed a ready and constant replenishment of soldiers.

Spartan men were preoccupied, obsessed even, with their military careers and, though usually marrying from their mid-twenties, did not see very much of domestic or family life before the age of thirty. Their wives played a vital economic role in raising their children and managing the household. It was they who were wholly responsible for raising sons until they were aged seven, when they left to join the junior army to begin their extensive and intensive training (*agoge*). It was, therefore, crucial that women of the citizen class be in tip-top condition physically and mentally for conception and motherhood. The wife stayed at home but was educated in the arts and took training in athletics, dancing and chariot racing. A strong, fit and educated mother delivered strong babies for a strong army.

Training for boys included testing endurance exercises and competitive sports. Combat training started at eighteen, all of which was designed to turn out troops of the highest fitness and caliber to fill the ranks of their crack units. Interestingly, exercises included special operations intelligence gathering against the lower-order serfs. Those serfs under surveillance who were deemed 'unsuitable' or 'inconvenient' in any way by the intelligence officers were winnowed out in an annual cull.

23. WOMEN ARE 'INCOMPLETE, DEFORMED MALES'

Of the sixty treatises written by the twenty or so Hippocratics, eleven cover gynaecology.

The Hippocratics believed that women's bodies comprised flesh that was softer and more porous than men's, an example being the female breast in which the woman's nourishment is converted into milk. This porosity was caused by the absorption of moisture in the form of blood, released each month during the woman's period. The concept of porosity is linked to the knowledge that women leak, through the vagina, with menstrual fluid, sexual lubricant, lochial discharge and discharges from various infections.

Blood clogging up the venous system in the breasts signifies that a woman is going mad – a physiological explanation for the age-old stereotype that women are naturally neurotic, erratic and unpredictable. Menstruation as a purging agent was, then, a good thing. Amenorrhœa caused all manner of physical and psychological illness; virgins were particularly susceptible, which explains their tendency to hang themselves or jump down wells to their deaths. In essence the physiological differences between men and women supported the belief that women were physically and mentally inferior to men.

Aristotle taught that men were more perfect than women; because they were less able than men to produce the heat that was vital for generation of the species – due to the debilitating effect of menstruation – women were incomplete, deformed males. In contrast to his Hippocratic contemporaries Aristotle believed that menstruation was not a good thing. Aristotle championed the long-standing myth that the womb comprised two separate compartments, often used to explain the birth of twins: males were born from the right (hotter) chamber, and females from the left, with all its sinister implications. He rejected the Hippocratic belief that hysteria in women was attributable to the movements of the womb and made tentative steps towards an understanding of the Fallopian tubes, largely unknown in antiquity.

Herophilus, in his *Midwifery*, differed from the Hippocratics in that he believed the womb to be no different from other internal organs. Herophilus was able to highlight the analogous relationship between the male testicles and the female ovaries; he believed that menstruation was the only physiological contribution women made to conception, and considered menstruation to be a cause of illness in women.

Causes of miscarriage can be found in the *Hippocratic Corpus*: carrying too heavy a weight, being beaten, jumping up into the air (an occupational hazard for dancers), lack of food and fainting, fear, loud shouting, flatulence and too much drink.

Women's medicine involved many remedies made up from various potions. Some of these were applied topically via salves and plasters; others were administered internally as fumigants, nasal clysters, enemas or pessaries. Fumigation involved the burning of agents such as human hair, medicinal herbs and bitumen in a pot. A lead tube was led from this into the woman's vagina. It was not without its hazards, if Soranus' warning about the dangers of burning the vagina is anything to go by. Enemas were introduced for disorders of the bladder, rectum, vagina and uterus – vaginal douches via vaginal clysters were often used.

24. Hysteria Was Central to Greek Gynaecology

Much of Greek gynaecology was focused on the womb (*hystera*) and woman's ability to bear children – the essential medical difference between men and women. Hippocrates puts it succinctly: 'the so-called women's diseases, the womb is the cause of them all'. Today, hysteria as a diagnosis or disorder is no longer recognised and has been replaced by 'histrionic personality disorder', which is associated with conditions such as social anxiety and schizophrenia – women have always been particularly prone, hence 'female hysteria'. Up until the late nineteenth century it was inextricably linked to movements of the womb, presenting as a lack of self-control caused by intense fear or anxiety often related to the imagined disease of a particular body part. Treatment was, for nearly two centuries, pelvic massage, in which the doctor stimulated the genitals until the patient achieved hysterical paroxysm, or orgasm.

The condition was thought to have been first noted around the time of the early Hippocratic writings and persisted as a diagnosis right through the Roman era. The Hippocratics never used the term *hysteria*; to them it was *pnix* – suffocation. They taught that the womb became dry if a woman did not have frequent sexual intercourse; infrequency would cause the womb to gravitate towards moister organs such as the liver, heart, brain, diaphragm or bladder, at which point the woman would faint, lose her voice and become 'hysterical'. The administration of sweet-smelling odours often restored the womb to its rightful place. Failing that, increasingly desperate measures involved binding the woman tightly beneath her breasts, palpating the affected organ, or hanging the woman upside down from a ladder.

Plato believed that an animal living inside a woman's womb was responsible for driving the maternal instinct to have children. If deprived of sexual activity, the animal became restless and wandered throughout the body causing apnea (difficulty in breathing) and other conditions and diseases. Sexual activity relieved the symptoms.

Hysteria was especially problematic in virgins and widows. Hippocrates warns that girls who delay marriage suffer nightmares from the time of their first period. This can result in them choking to death: the blood in their womb cannot escape because the cervix is still intact and so it flows back up to the heart and lungs, driving the woman mad. Fever ensues, accompanied by a tendency for suicide caused by the nightmares; these encourage the woman to jump down wells or to hang themselves. Hippocrates' advice is for girls in such a condition to lose their virginity; they will be cured when they fall pregnant. Widows, similarly, are cured by sex, or just by climaxing, so that the retained female semen can be released. The inevitable conclusion was that, deprived of sex, a woman would go mad, and the best way to preserve one's sanity was to have sex, and to have it often.

The only real cure, then, for the 'hysterical' woman, was to become pregnant – thus conveniently enabling the woman to fulfil her role as a wife, as well as satisfying her husband's needs for sexual gratification.

25. Greek Gods and Goddesses Reflected All Human Life

We have already met some of the members of the Greek pantheon. Here are a number of lesser deities, illustrating just how pervasive they were, representing and mirroring all aspects of human life down on Earth:

Aeolus – God of the winds.

Amphitrite – Queen of the sea, mother of Triton and wife of Poseidon.

Aura – Goddess of breezes and fresh air.

Circe – Minor goddess of magic (not to be confused with Hecate).

Eileithyia – Goddess of childbirth, daughter of Hera and Zeus.

Eris – Goddess of discord and strife.

Ganymede – Cup-bearer of the gods on Olympus.

The Three Graces – Goddesses of beauty and attendants of Aphrodite and Hera.

Hecate – Goddess of magic, witches and crossroads.

Helios – Titan, personification of the sun.

Hypnos – God of sleep, father of Morpheus and son of Nyx.

The Moirai – The 'Fates': **Clotho** (the spinner), **Lachesis** (the allotter) and **Atropos** (the unturnable).

Morpheus – God of dreams.

The Muses – Nine goddesses of science and arts: **Calliope, Urania, Clio, Polyhymnia, Melpomene, Terpsichore, Thalia, Euterpe,** and **Erato.**

Nemesis – Greek goddess of retribution and revenge, daughter of Nyx.

Nike – Goddess of victory.

Perseus – Son of Zeus and Danae, slayer of Medusa, the legendary founder of Mycenae and of the Perseid dynasty.

Selene – Titaness, personification of the moon.

Styx – Goddess of the infernal River Styx, the river in which gods swear oaths.

Thanatos – God of death, and sometimes a personification of death.

Theseus – Son of Poseidon, first hero of Athens and slayer of the Minotaur.

Triton – Messenger of the seas, son of Poseidon and Amphitrite.

Tyche – Goddess of luck.

26. THAT TO PRODUCE A MALE CHILD RAPID THRUSTING DURING SEX AT THE END OF THE WOMAN'S PERIOD WAS NECESSARY

Hippocrates gives us some intriguing gynaecological case studies: a woman from Pheres suffered from idiopathic headache, which persisted even after her skull was drained; during her period the headache was less severe. The headaches stopped when she became pregnant, suggesting that the time-honoured excuse for declining sex is not always the best way to a good night's sleep. A woman from Larissa suffered pain during intercourse (dyspareunia); when she reached sixty, she felt what she thought were severe labour pains after eating lots of leeks. She stood up and felt something in her vagina, and fainted. Another woman pulled out what appeared to be the whorl of a spindle. Hippocrates records that the woman made a full recovery; one wonders if the other woman ever did...

On conception, to produce a male child rapid thrusting during sex at the end of the woman's period is recommended; for a girl things are slightly less vigorous or spontaneous and involve tying up the right testicle for sex in the middle of the period.

Contraception was somewhat makeshift. Aristotle had advocated smearing cedar oil, white lead or frankincense on the female genitals while the *Hippocratic Corpus* swore by drinking *misy* – dilute copper sulphate. Greek courtesans, or *hetaerae,* frequently practiced male-female anal intercourse as a means of avoiding pregnancy.

To the ancient Greeks sexual orientation was not a social identifier as it is in modern Western societies. Greek (and Roman) society was not obsessed with sexual desire or behaviour according to gender, but was rather more concerned with the role that the participants played in the sex act – essentially, whether they were an active penetrator or being passively penetrated. This active-passive role corresponded with dominant and submissive social roles: the active penetrative role assumed masculinity, higher social status, and adulthood, while the passive role was akin to femininity, lower social status, and youth.

The Sacred Band of Thebes, what we might call Special Forces, was a military unit made up only of men and their male lovers, and is the best example there is of how the ancient Greeks used love and sex between soldiers to boost morale.

'Greek love' is sometimes used to refer to anal intercourse, and nowadays even, 'doing it the Greek way' is still used to denote anal sex. To the ancient Greeks romantic and sexual relationships between males was indicative of a balanced sex life, having men and women as lovers. This was considered quite normal so long as one partner was an adult and the other was aged between twelve and fifteen.

Nevertheless, male-male anal sex was not as common as is often thought; Aristophanes, for example, mocks the practice, claiming, 'Most citizens are *europroktoi* (wide-arsed) now.' The terms *kinaidos*, *europroktoi*, and *katapygon* were used by Greeks to vilify men who habitually indulged in passive anal intercourse. More respectably to the Greeks, pedagogic pederasty was an essential element in the education of male adolescents, but these relationships often avoided penetrative sex.

27. Pericles Was Largely Responsible for Much of the Construction on the Acropolis

If there is one single, truly iconic symbol of all things ancient Greek it is the Acropolis and the magnificent Parthenon that dominate the city of Athens – and Western civilization generally.

Acropolis comes from the Greek words ἄκρον ('edge', or 'extremity') and πόλις (polis, 'city'). The Acropolis was rebuilt in white marble from 449 BC; work on the Parthenon began in 447 BC and was completed in 456. It was dedicated to Athena Nike (patron goddess of the city) and houses a huge statue of the goddess. The Erechtheum, with its caryatids, marble female figures, supporting the roof, and the Temple of Athena Nike were built on the Acropolis at the same time. Pericles (c. 495–429 BC) was largely responsible for much of the construction on the Acropolis.

Access was through the Propylaea, a large gateway building (437–432). The Theatre of Dionysus, at the southern base of the Acropolis, was the city's theatre (330), rubbing shoulders with shrines to Asclepius and Dionysus. The city was connected to the port of Piraeus by the parallel Long Walls, which formed a corridor 550 feet wide.

What we see today was not, of course, the first and only construction on the Acropolis. There was a Doric temple to Athena Polias from around 570–550 BC, referred to as the Hekatompedon or Ur-Parthenon ('original Parthenon'). The Pisistratids built another temple between 529–520 BC – the Old Temple of Athena (Arkhaios Neōs (ἀρχαῖος νεώς), destroyed in the Persian invasion in 480 BC. Around 500 BC the Ur-Parthenon was dismantled to make place for the 'Older Parthenon' (the Pre-Parthenon). This was still under construction when the Persians sacked the city in 480 BC. After their victory at Eurymedon in 468 BC, Cimon and Themistocles commissioned the reconstruction of the southern and northern walls of the Acropolis. Most of the major temples, including the Parthenon, were rebuilt under Pericles during what is called the Golden Age of Athens (460–430 BC). Phidias, Ictinus and Callicrates were responsible for this reconstruction.

Other important buildings in classical Athens were the Agora (originally from the sixth century), the civic centre – the hub of political, commercial and cultural life. The Agora contained two *stoas*, or long colonnaded halls, and the Theseum. It was near to the Areopagus, seat of the high court, and the Pnyx (*ekklesia*), where the Athenian assembly convened with its *bema* – the speaker's platform hewn out of the rock.

In the Byzantine age, the Parthenon became a church dedicated to the Virgin Mary. Under the Latin Duchy of Athens, the Acropolis was the city's administrative hub, with the Parthenon its cathedral, and the Propylaia as part of the Ducal Palace.

With the Ottoman conquest of Greece, the Parthenon was used as the garrison headquarters of the Turkish army, and the Erechtheum became the Governor's harem. In 1687 the Acropolis suffered during the siege by the Venetians: the Parthenon, then a gunpowder magazine, was hit by artillery fire and was severely damaged.

28. THE AMAZONS HAVE NO RIGHT BREASTS

The only sure thing that can be said about the Amazons is that nothing about them can be said for sure. Controversy or speculation surrounds every aspect of them. In Greek mythology, the Amazons (Ἀμαζόνες) were redoubtable woman warriors. Herodotus believed them to be related to the Scythians and located them somewhere between Scythia and Sarmatia (roughly modern Ukraine). Others have them in Pontus, Anatolia on the River Don, or Libya. The Greeks called the Don Tanais, but the Scythians called it the 'Amazon'.

The most famous of the Amazons was Penthesilea, who fought in the Trojan War, and her sister Hippolyta, whose magic girdle, given to her by her father Ares, god of war, was the ninth labour that exercised Hercules. Hippolyta was the founding queen – her name means unbridled mare. The Greeks had a word for battle with Amazons – *amazonomachy*. Their name is a byword for female warriors in general. Amazons were said to have founded many cities including Smyrna, Paphos, Ephesus and Magnesia, and as horse-born fighters they are also credited with inventing the cavalry.

The accidental hunting accident death of Hippolyta by Penthesilea led to her own death at the hands of Achilles. Penthesilea was so distraught that she wished only to die, but, because she was an Amazon, only honorably so and in battle. According to Quintus Smyrnaeus' *Posthomerica*, she readily joined in the Trojan War on the side of Troy, promising that she would slay Achilles. She eventually confronted the Greek who, with only one blow, knocked her to the ground; she begged for mercy but Achilles was unmoved and killed her, scoffing at her corpse – until he removed her helmet. It was at this point that he felt remorse for his actions.

The etymology of Amazon is disputed: it may be from a Greek word meaning 'without men or husbands', or alternatively it may be from ἀ- and μαζός, 'without breast', reflecting an etiological tradition that Amazons cut off their right breast. Greek art does not support this, as the Amazons are always depicted with both breasts intact. Hippocrates differs: 'They have no right breasts ... for while they are yet babies their mothers make red-hot a bronze instrument constructed for this very purpose and apply it to the right breast and cauterize it, so that its growth is arrested, and all its strength and bulk are diverted to the right shoulder and right arm.'

If the Amazons lived without men and they were 'really killers of men' (*androktones*), as Herodotus would have us believe, how then did they survive? Once a year they visited the neighbouring Gargareans and had sex with them. Any resulting male children were either killed, sent back to their fathers or exposed. The girls, however, were retained and raised by their mothers with training in agriculture, hunting, and combat. Others say that when the Amazons went to war they would spare some of the men and take them as sex slaves, having sex with them to produce their girls.

29. THE FIRST OLYMPIC GAMES TOOK PLACE IN 776 BC

The ancient Olympic Games were held in Olympia from 776 BC to 393 AD. They were four-yearly religious and athletic festivals held at the sanctuary of Zeus and they lasted for five days. Competition was between city-states and featured athletic and combat sports such as wrestling and the *pankration*, and horse and chariot racing events. There is no truth in the belief that during the games all conflicts among the participants were suspended until the games were finished. This fictitious cessation of hostilities was known as the Olympic peace or truce.

It all started with Heracles who, having discharged his twelve labours, built the Olympic Stadium in honour of Zeus; then he walked in a straight line for 200 steps and called this distance a *stadion*, which later became a unit of distance and an event – a sprint of around 200 metres. The ancient games featured running events, a pentathlon (a jumping event, discus and javelin, a foot race, and wrestling), boxing, wrestling, *pankration*, a race in armour and equestrian events. Coroebus, a cook from Elis, was apparently the first Olympic champion. The prize was a crown of wild olive (*kotinos*).

In long jump athletes used stone or lead weights (*halteres*) to lengthen their jumps. They held onto the weights until the end of their leap when they jettisoned them to propel themselves forward. *Pankration* was a primitive martial art combining wrestling and boxing and was one of the toughest sports. The Greeks believed that it was invented by Theseus when he overcame the Minotaur in the labyrinth.

Any free, male Greek citizen was entitled to participate in the games regardless of their social status. Orsippos, a general from Megara; Polymnistor, a shepherd; Diagoras, a member of a royal family from Rhodes; Alexander I, son of Amyndas and King of Macedonia; and Democritus, a philosopher, were all participants in the games. Married women were not permitted to participate in nor watch the games. However, unmarried women were allowed to attend as spectators, and the priestess of Demeter, goddess of fertility, was given a privileged seat.

Kyniska, daughter of King Archidamus of Sparta, was the first woman to go down as an Olympic victor. Her chariot won in the four-horse chariot race in the 96th and 97th Olympiads (396 BC and 392 BC respectively). It was of course forbidden for women to compete, but in the equestrian events, the victory wreath was awarded to the owner, not the rider, of the horse.

Astylos of Croton won no less than six victory olive wreaths in three Olympiads (488–480 BC) in the *stade* and the *diaulos* (twice the *stade*) events. In the first Olympiad, he ran for Croton and his compatriots duly honoured and glorified him. However, in the next two Olympiads he competed as a citizen of Syracuse. The people of Croton punished him by demolishing his statue and turning his house into a prison.

30. Charon is a Euphemism for Death

The underworld and life after death were just as important to the superstitious Greeks as life itself and the living world. Charon, the unkempt and grumpy ferryman, has a long and not very illustrious history – you met him as you clamoured with hordes of other recently dead anxious to get over the murky underworld river. Conditions were not good: there were urgent crowds pressing in on you, the ferryman was churlish and repellent, and the gloomy boat leaked. Moreover, some say you had to help with the rowing, and everyone had to have the right change ready. No obol, no ride.

Charon's credentials were excellent. He was the son of brother and sister Nyx (night) and Erebus (darkness). He was the brother of Thanatos (death) and Hypnos (sleep). His name comes from χαρωπός (*charopós*), 'he of the keen gaze', and reflects his piercing, laser-like eyes. Charon is a euphemism for death.

The celebrated Charon episodes in *Aeneid* 6 (298–304; 384–416) are built from a number of Greek sources that provided Virgil with a rich fund of material to work from. Despite his absence from Homer's *Odyssey*, Charon had already become a stock figure in epic poetry by the fifth century BC. He was a key character in the epic underworld with its supernatural, chthonic elements, itself a traditional feature of epic in antiquity.

The first source comes from the travel writer and geographer Pausanias (*c.* AD 110–AD 180), who mentions the lost *Minyad*, written around or soon after the time of Homer, as being a possible source for a painting in the Lesche of the Cnidians at Delphi by Polygnotus (mid-fifth century BC), which featured scenes of the underworld.

In the fifth century a fragment of Pindar's describes the scene at the end of the infernal crossing: 'But they, set free from sickness and old age and toils, having fled from the deeply sounding ferry of Acheron.' The sombre environment in which Charon works is vividly portrayed by Aeschylus in his *Seven Against Thebes*. Euripides, in the *Alcestis*, takes up the characteristic grumpiness: '*Alcestis*: I can see him there with the oars of his little boat in the lake, the ferryman of the dead, Charon, hand on oar; he shouts over to me: "What are you waiting for? Hurry, you're holding us up." He urges me on, angry, impatient.' Charon takes centre stage in Aeschylus' *Frogs*. He is a comedic figure here, of course: ancient and old, his boat is impossibly tiny, his fare is an inflated two obols, he is rude, the passengers have to share with the rowing, there is a no-slave policy and the voyage is serenaded by the chorus of frogs.

Plato, in the *Phaedo* (112e), describes Charon's situation, and in a lost *katabasis* describing an underworld journey by Orpheus. Servius notes that Charon is frightened into allowing a very alive Heracles cross the Styx to capture Cerberus. He is shackled for a year as punishment.

31. Cynisca Won the Four-Horse Race in 396 and 392 BC

As important as the role of the Spartan woman was, some took it one stage further and carved out a life of exceptional achievement and determination. As we have seen, Cynisca from the early fourth century was the wealthy daughter of the king of Sparta, Archidamus II. Xenophon tells us that she was urged by her brother, Agesilaus II, to compete in the Olympic Games in the prestigious four-horse chariot race as an owner and trainer of horses. Agesilaus was always keen to instill bravery and belligerence in the Spartans. Cynisca duly won the four-horse race in 396 BC and in 392 BC. She was honoured with a bronze statue of a chariot and horses, a charioteer and a statue in the Temple of Zeus in Olympia. The inscription read that she was the only woman to win in the chariot events at the Olympic Games. Other female Spartan and Greek chariot race winners include Euryleonis, Belistiche, Timareta, Theodota and Cassia. Spartan Euryleonis was victorious in the two-horse chariot races in the 368 BC games. Belistiche was a courtesan, a *hetaira*; she won the four-horse (*tethrippon*) and two-horse (*synoris*) races in the 264 BC Olympic Games. Ptolemy II Philadelphus was so impressed that he took her as his mistress and deified her as Aphrodite Belistiche. According to Clement of Alexandria, she was buried under the Shrine of Sarapis in Alexandria.

32. Sappho Was Commonly Regarded in Antiquity as One of the Greatest Lyric Poets and Was Called 'The Tenth Muse'

Sappho was a Greek lyric poet (*c.* 620–570 BC) born on Lesbos. Her poetry was well known and admired but most has been lost. Nevertheless her reputation endures through surviving fragments. Sappho was commonly regarded in antiquity as one of the greatest lyric poets and was called 'the tenth muse'. Details of her life are sketchy. One story going back to Menander (Fr. 258 K) says that Sappho committed suicide by jumping off the Leucadian Cliffs for love of Phaon, a ferryman. An attempt to heterosexualise her? She was probably married and had a daughter, Cleis.

Sappho focuses on love for various people of both sexes. Of the 12,000 lines of poetry she is thought to have composed, many of which described her love for other women, only around 600 lines have survived. As a result of her fame in antiquity, she and her island have become emblematic of love between women. Our word lesbian derives from Lesbos, while her name is also the origin of the word sapphic; neither word was applied to female homosexuality until 1890.

Sappho is also believed to have been in charge of what was known as a *thiasos* – a community in which Greek girls could receive a basic education and, at the same time, were exposed to homosexual love, sometimes for their teachers (Sappho writes of her love for various students) and sometimes for each other. As the *polis* evolved, however, marriage became established as a social norm and women were confined to their houses, bringing an end to the *thiasoi* and with it much of Athenian female homosexuality, which had no place within the constraints of this new social organization.

Sappho's contemporary, Alcaeus, described her as 'Violet-haired, pure, honey-smiling Sappho' – (Fr. 384).

Of the 200 fragments of Sappho's poetry, *Fragment 16* and *Fragment 44* are lyric retellings of Homer. Both allude to scenes in the *Iliad*, which Sappho expands on: *Fragment 16* characterises Helen, while *44* describes the domestic joy leading up to the wedding of Hector and Andromache.

Sappho's reception down the ages has been sadly hijacked by moralists, most of whom have missed the finer points of her verse. The Poetry Foundation puts it well:

Much of the history of Sappho's reputation, though, is the story of her appropriation by moralists. Those New Comedians who picked up the strain of abuse initiated by the Anacreontic fragment mentioned earlier rendered the poet a popular burlesque comic figure on the stage. A good many plays centered around Sappho, though most were wholly unrelated to her life or her poetry. Later Christian censors in various ages in Alexandria, Rome, and Constantinople condemned her in words such as those of Tatian, who called her 'a whore who sang about her own licentiousness'. Saint Gregory of Nazianzus and Pope Gregory VII ordered her works burned.

http://www.poetryfoundation.org/bio/sappho
accessed 16 December 2015

Parts of two previously unknown poems by Sappho were published in February 2014 in the *Times Literary Supplement*.

33. Draco Gives Us Our Word 'Draconian' to Describe Repressive Legal Measures

Draco lived sometime during the seventh century BC. History remembers him as the Athenian lawgiver whose unforgiving and harsh legal code punished both trivial and serious crimes alike with death – hence our word draconian, to describe repressive legal measures. Aristotle in his *Constitution of Athens* tells us about the six junior archons (*thesmotetai*), or magistrates, instituted in Athens after 683 BC to record the laws. If this is so, Draco's code of 621 was not the first written transcription of Athenian law in writing, as is often supposed. But it may be the first comprehensive written code; it replaced the existing system of oral law and blood feud with a written code to be enforced only by a court. Solon, archon in 594 BC, later repealed Draco's legislation and published new laws, keeping only Draco's statutes on murder, which distinguished between murder and manslaughter. Apparently, Draco met his death in the Aeginetan theatre when his supporters 'threw so many hats and shirts and cloaks on his head that he suffocated, and was buried in that same theatre'.

Examples of Draconian laws are a debtor whose status was lower than that of his creditor being reduced to slavery – a more lenient punishment awaited those in debt to a member of the lower orders. Even more savage was the death penalty meted out to anyone stealing a cabbage. Demades, the fourth-century orator, said that Draco wrote laws in blood, not ink.

34. SOLON UNDID ALL OF DRACO'S BAD WORK

As we have seen, Solon undid all of Draco's bad work. To Herodotus he was sage, lawgiver and poet. Thucydides ignores him. History remembers Solon for his efforts to legislate against political, economic and moral malaise in Athens and is often credited with laying the foundations for Athenian democracy and establishing stability in classical Athens.

Solon was a great reformer. Having been awarded dictatorial powers, he tackled head on the socially unjust situation in Athens, which favoured the aristocracy, the *eupatridae*, who possessed the best land and monopolized the higher echelons of government despite being riven by divisive rival factions. Poorer farmers were driven into debt by them and, as noted, were enslaved when they defaulted. There was obviously much resentment among farmers, artisans and merchants, which could well have resulted in revolution and tyranny as in other Greek states.

His economic reforms included the 'shaking off of burdens' (*seisachtheia*), in which he returned to their owners all forfeited land and freed all the citizens enslaved under Draco. What he did not do, and what the poorer farmers really wanted, was carry out a wholesale land distribution.

He banned all loans secured on the borrower's person and introduced measures to increase overall prosperity, stimulate the economy and provide alternative occupations in the trades and professions for those unable to live by farming. This was to be done through fathers for their sons: if the fathers failed in this, they forfeited the legal requirement for sons to look after their fathers in old age. Only olive oil and black figure pottery could now be exported with an embargo on grain, so much of which had hitherto been exported that it led to a domestic shortage. Poverty, though never eliminated, loosened the grip it had on Attica before Solon's reforms.

On the political front, Solon abolished the monopoly of the *eupatridae* and replaced it with government by the wealthy citizens, establishing a census of annual income based on measures of grain, oil, and wine, and divided the citizens into four income groups. All citizens qualified to attend the general Assembly (*ekklesia*), which theoretically became the sovereign body with powers to enact laws, elect officials, and hear appeals from the courts (the *Heliaia*). All but the very poorest (the *thetes*) could now serve for one year at a time on the newly created Council of Four Hundred, which was a kind of steering committee for the Assembly. The more senior government posts were reserved for citizens of the top two income groups. Although a powerful conservative element persisted in the Council of the Hill of Ares (Areopagus), and the people themselves (equally conservative) still preferred to entrust the most important offices to the old aristocratic families, Solon laid the foundations of the future democracy in Athens.

Finally, Solon, as noted, repealed all of Draco's draconian legislation, other than those laws relating to homicide. Solon was the first of the Athenian poets whose work has survived to the present day, albeit in fragmentary form.

35. Solon Had a Profound Influence on Athenian Sexual Mores

Solon is less well known for his influence on Athenian sexual mores. If a fragment from a play called *Brothers* by the comic playwright Philemon is to believed, Solon set up state-run brothels in the city in order to democratize the pleasures of sex. Some ancient authors assert that Solon regulated pederastic relationships in Athens when he allegedly drew up statutes intended to promote and safeguard pederasty and to control abuses against freeborn boys. The orator Aeschines cites laws banning slaves from wrestling halls and forbidding them to enter pederastic relationships with the sons of citizens. Others infer that Solon had a vested interest in all of this, citing as evidence the fact that Solon had taken the tyrant-in-waiting Peisistratos as his *eromenos*. Aristotle, in his *Athenian Constitution* written around 330 BC, was having none of it though, claiming that 'those are manifestly talking nonsense who pretend that Solon was the lover of Peisistratos, for their ages do not admit of it'. Solon was around thirty years older than Peisistratos. Plutarch (*c.* AD 46–AD 120), however, was less than convinced by Aristotle. This is from his biography of Solon: 'And they say Solon loved [Peisistratos]; and that is the reason, I suppose, that when afterwards they differed about the government, their enmity never produced any hot and violent passion, they remembered their old kindnesses, and retained "Still in its embers living the strong fire" of their love and dear affection.'

Aelian (*c.* AD 175–*c.* 235) also believed that Peisistratos had been Solon's *eromenos*.

Solon's alleged pederastic leanings were thought in antiquity to be reflected in his poetry, or rather a few surviving fragments thereof. However, the authenticity of these is uncertain and may have been by Theognis instead.

Another law reported by Plutarch in the *Life of Solon* decreed: 'that the bride and bridegroom shall be shut into a chamber, and eat a quince together; and that the husband of an heiress shall have sex with her three times a month; for though there be no children, yet it is an honour and due affection which a husband ought to pay to a virtuous, chaste wife; it removes all petty differences, and will not permit their little quarrels to proceed to a divorce'.

He forbade dowries, and he would not have marriages contracted for gain or land, but only for pure love, kind affection, and the birth of children.

He regulated women's walks, feasts, and displays of mourning and banned everything that was either unbecoming or immodest; no more than three articles of dress were permitted; an obol's worth of meat and drink; and no basket higher than a cubit; and at night they were only allowed out in a chariot preceded by a torch. Sacrificing an ox at the grave was not allowed.

36. THE GREEK MAGICAL PAPYRI ARE A VERITABLE VADE MECUM OF POTIONS AND SPELLS

Generally, the ancient Greeks – like the Egyptians before them and the Romans after them – were, by nature, very superstitious. The dark arts have been dabbled in for as long as religions have been practised, in all societies. Ancient Greece is no exception.

One of the most fertile sources of this information comes from Egypt, in the shape of the *Papyri Graecae Magicae*, the *Greek Magical Papyri*. This astonishing body of work is a veritable *vade mecum* of potions and spells, arcane occult knowledge and recipes for magical concoctions accumulated over the centuries. In addition, we have the *voces magicae* and the *Ephesia Grammata*: Greek magic formulae made up of unintelligible words – mumbo jumbo – which were chanted to ward off evil, and hordes of magical *ostraca*, the damning-to-hell *tabellae defixionum*, curse tablets, voodoo dolls, love philtres, amulets and phylacteries, etched with magical formulae.

One thousand six hundred or so curse tablets have been found – *defixiones* or *katadesies*, curse tablets or binding spells. Predominantly a practice of the lower orders, the curses were often provoked by an unfortunate turn of events such as commercial disputes, lawsuits, or unrequited and spurned love. They gave vent to the curser's vengeful anger, jealousy, malice and vindictiveness. Here is one example: 'I bind you, Theodotis, daughter of Eus, to the snake's tail, the crocodile's mouth, the ram's horns, the asp's poison, the cat's whiskers, the god's appendage, so that you may never be able to have sex with another man, not be shagged or be buggered or give a blow job, nor do anything that brings you pleasure with another man, unless I alone, Ammonion, the son of Hermitaris, am that man... Make this erotic binding-spell work, so that Theodotis, may no longer be penetrated by a man other than me alone, Ammonion, the son of Hermitaris, dragged in slavery, driven crazy, taking to the air in search of Ammonion, the son of Hermitaris, and that she may rub her thigh on my thigh, her genitals to my genitals, for sex with me for the rest of her life.'

Trade and commercial competition, then as now, brought out the worst in people. The precedent is set by a very early curse in the Hesiodic hexameter poem *Kiln*, in which aptly named demons are invoked against rival potters leaving nothing to chance, the angry dedicator invoking these demons, weapons of mass destruction: 'may the entire kiln be throw into and may the potters wail at length. Just as the horse's jaw grinds, may the kiln also grind all the pots within it reducing them to fragments... May they smash these works up, and destroy the kiln. May the potters themselves witness these terrible deeds and lament. If any of them peer into the kiln, may fire scorch his whole face, so that they may all learn to treat people fairly'.

37. Peisistratus Was Tyrant in 560 BC

If ever there was a real-world illustration of the truism that you cannot please all the people all of the time, or some people are never happy, then the reforms of Solon provide that illustration. Having delivered the majority of Athenians from abject and deepening poverty and enslavement, Solon received no thanks. In trying to please everyone, he had pleased no one. Instead, the dissatisfaction opened the door for Peisistratus to enter the stage as tyrant in 560 BC. Solon's laws were set in stone for 100 years (or rather wood because they were committed to large wooden slabs or attached to a series of axles called *axones* that stood in the Prytaneion) and he set off on ten years of travel soon after their enactment. When he returned, however, he found rival factions at each other's throats and Peisistratus, his friend, waiting in the wings.

Tyranny apart, Peisistratus is remembered as the founder of the Panathenaic Festival, in 566 BC, and for an early attempt to produce a definitive version of the Homeric epics. The first Great Panathenaea was based on the Olympic Games, but Peisistratos added music and poetry competitions. Chariot racing was the most prestigious event, unlike the Olympics where the *stadion* (foot race) was most important.

Peisistratus rose to fame after capturing the port of Nisaea in Megara in a coup in 564 BC. After this, three factions vied for power in Athens: Lycurgus led the Pedieis, the people who lived on the plains producing grain, giving them power during the food shortage; the Paralioi lived along the coast, led by Megakles, who controlled the sea and much of Athens' trade; the Hyperakrioi were hill people and easily the poorest of the Athenians, bartering in honey and wool. Peisistratus organized this faction – they easily outnumbered the other two parties put together.

With the support of Megakles, Peisistratus declared himself tyrant. It was never plain sailing, though: Peisistratos was removed from office and exiled twice during his reign. The first time was around 555 BC but when the Pedieis and the Paralioi fell out, Peisistratos returned to Athens, entering the city in spectacular fashion in a golden chariot with a tall female Athena-lookalike. Many came back to him in the belief that he had the favour of the goddess. During his second exile, he acquired resources from the Laurion silver mines near Athens and, after ten years, he returned in force as tyrant until his death in 527 BC.

Peisistratus' salient policies, like those of Solon, were aimed at reinforcing the economy. He offered land and loans to the poor, and he encouraged the cultivation of olives and stimulated Athenian trade, establishing routes to the Black Sea, Italy and France. Peisistratus' public building projects provided jobs for the unemployed while making the city a cultural hub. He replaced the private wells of the aristocrats with public fountain houses and built the first aqueduct in Athens, opening a reliable water supply for the population for the first time.

38. Greek Tyranny Was Not Necessarily a Bad Thing

In ancient Greece the word tyrant, like the Roman word dictator, did not always have the sinister connotations it has today. Far from being violent and oppressive, Peisistratus' tyranny was economically productive and fair and, in that, was fairly typical: he seized power as an aristocrat with the support of disaffected members of the community; his rule was benign, the reign was relatively short term, usually supplanted by another generation of malcontents behind a new tyrant. The tyrant could be malevolent or just as easily benevolent, malign or benign. He was never a Domitian or a Hitler. Herodotus said that Peisistratos, 'not having disturbed the existing magistrates nor changed the ancient laws ... administered the State under that constitution of things which was already established, ordering it fairly and well'. Aristotle believed that 'his administration was temperate ... and more like constitutional government than a tyranny'. Peisistratos tried to distribute power and benefits, intent on easing tensions between the economic classes. For the lower order, he cut taxes and formed a band of travelling judges to dispense justice for the citizens.

Culturally, he did much for Athens. He minted coins bearing Athena's owl symbol, while two new forms of poetry, the dithyramb and Attic tragedy, were created during a period of growth in theatre, arts, and sculpture. In short, Peisitratus beautified Athens. As noted, he commissioned the permanent copying and archiving of Homer's *Iliad* and the *Odyssey*. Plato and Aristotle both deplored tyranny as a form of constitution.

39. Male Bisexuality Was Widely Tolerated

The chapter on Sappho dealt with female homosexuality. Attitudes to what we term homosexuality were very different in the ancient world. For example, there are no words in Greek or Latin for homosexual or heterosexual, which may suggest that *the difference* did not exercise the Greeks and Romans in the same way as it has troubled other societies in the last 2,000 years. As we have seen, sexual orientation seems to have been largely irrelevant; indeed, such words as pornography, homosexual and lesbian are nineteenth century in origin. As in Rome, it was the role the adult homosexual played in physical homoerotic love that was crucial – not the fact that the partners were homosexual. Allowing one's body to be exploited for pleasure by others in sodomy and oral sex was a sign of weakness, a deficiency of masculinity. It was fine, however, for a man to indulge with males lower down the social ladder – male prostitutes or slaves – so long as he assumed the penetrative role and was in no way passive or submissive. Penetration was manly and powerful; passivity was weak and effeminate – something that women and slaves did that was stigmatic and attracted prejudice.

Eva Cantarella describes the situation best, pointing out that male bisexuality was widely tolerated and ruled by law, and generally not stigmatised by the public: 'homosexuality was not an exclusive choice. Loving another man was not an option out of the norm, different, somehow deviant. It was just a part of life experience; it was the show of an either sentimental or sexual drive that, over a lifetime, alternated and was associated (sometimes at the very same time) with love for a woman.' (*Bisexuality in the Ancient World 2nd Edition*, 2002 trans. Cormac O' Cuilleanain.)

Adult male couples include Pausanias (*fl. c.* 420 BC) and the thirty-year-old tragic poet Agathon, and Alexander the Great and his boyhood friend Hephaestion. Agathon hosts a banquet, described in Plato's *Symposium*, at which the theme for discussion is love, and in which Pausanias plays a leading role. Pausanias draws a distinction between a higher and lower kind of love: all the base lover wants is sexual gratification, and his objects are women and boys. The noble lover aims at young men, with whom he establishes lifelong relationships founded on respecting one's partner's intelligence. Diogenes Laertius wrote that Alcibiades, the Athenian general and politician of the fifth century BC, 'in his adolescence he drew away the husbands from their wives, and as a young man the wives from their husbands'. Of the general Hephaestion (*c.* 356 BC–324 BC), Curtius tells us that he was 'by far the dearest of all the king's friends; he had been brought up with Alexander and shared all his secrets', although this could simply mean that they were just very good friends.

There were, however, regional variations in the attitude towards same-sex love. For example, in parts of Ionia there was general disapproval while in Elis and Boiotia it was approved of, even celebrated.

40. Pederasty Was the Sexual Pursuit of Boys by Men

Paiderastia is the Greek word for the sexual pursuit of boys by men. This was a relationship between an older male and a boy, a boy being a 'boy' until he sported a full beard, at which point he became a man. Pederasty then usually extended from around twelve years of age to around seventeen. The older man was the *erastes*, and his role was to educate, protect, love, provide moral improvement for and be a role model for his *eromenos*.

The tradition emanates from when tribal communities were organized in age groups. When a boy was on the threshold of becoming a man, he would go off with an older man, who would school the youth in the ways of Greek life and the responsibilities of adulthood, a rite of passage which endured into and through the age of the *polis*. Education apart, this was also a sexual relationship with the critical proviso that penetrative sex was often banned as it was considered demeaning for the passive partner and socially unacceptable. Penetration, such as it was, was therefore intercrural (between the boy's thighs) rather than anal or oral. Pederasty also served to highlight the distinction between physical love (*eros*) and non-sexual love (*philia*): the man could demonstrate sexual desire, *eros*, but not the boy, on the grounds that if he enjoyed penetration he was acting as a pathic, a *kinaedos* or catamite – weak and womanlike. Women were routinely penetrated and they were socially and politically inferior.

There was a cooling-off period at the start of the relationship when the young object of desire rebuffed all advances until such time he could be sure of the good intentions of the *erastes* and that he was not just pursuing him out of lust. Plutarch's quotation from Philip II may be confirmation of the prevalence of pederasty: 'It is not only the most warlike peoples, the Boeotians, Spartans, and Cretans, who are the most susceptible to this kind of love but also the greatest heroes of old: Meleager, Achilles, Aristomenes, Cimon, and Epaminondas.'

Theocritus, Achilles Tatius, and Solon all celebrate homosexuality. Solon writes in his *Boys and Sport*: 'Blest is the man who loves and after early play Whereby his limbs are supple made and strong Retiring to his house with wine and song Toys with a fair boy on his breast the livelong day!'

Two of Plato's works, *The Phaedrus* and *The Symposium*, give us a picture of contemporary attitudes toward pederasty. At the beginning of *The Phaedrus*, Phaedrus and Socrates are discussing a speech that Lysias, an orator, has written; a speech that was '...designed to win over a handsome boy...'. Socrates states that man 'cannot have a less desirable protector or companion than the man who is in love with him'. *The Symposium* goes into even greater detail, where several men all give speeches about why a love of boys is a good thing.

41. ARISTOPHANES SCORNS THE IDEA OF A VISIT TO THE UNDERWORLD

In the fifth century the satirical playwright Aristophanes pokes fun at the idea of visiting the underworld. In the *Frogs*, he has the wine-god Dionysus going down to the kingdom of Hades to rescue Semele, his mother. In his *Plutus*, Aristophanes scorns magicians. In another of his plays, the *Clouds*, Strepsiades and the philosopher Socrates debate whether to buy a Thessalian witch (*pharmakis*) to help them draw down the moon and lock it away so that Strepsiades can avoid interest payments on his debts.

Sophocles takes witchcraft more seriously. He describes Medea in the *Rhizotomoi* as she harvests her roots naked, her hair in disarray, and the other 'root-cutters' of the play's title are a chorus of witches. In his *Oedipus Tyrannus* Sophocles uses the character of Creon to elaborately and at some length describe the setting for a necromancy in which a multitude of ghosts are summoned. Later, Oedipus verbally abuses the prophetic Tiresias, calling him 'a schemer, a peddler of fraudulent tricks', questioning his motives, his professionalism and his ability as a seer.

Aeschylus' chorus of Persians raises the ghost of their former king Darius I. The ghost foretells the doom awaiting Xerxes' expedition to conquer Greece. Aeschylus has a chorus of evocators (*psuchagogoi* – summoners of ghosts) who raise the souls of the night wanderers around the mouth of the Styx (probably at Lake Avernus), after sacrificial blood has seeped down to them. The scene is parodied in Aristophanes' *Birds*, where a camel is the sacrificial victim and the necromancy produces nothing but a bat.

The other great fifth-century playwright, Euripides, has his *Medea*. He alludes to evocators who summon the dead when he describes how Heracles' restored to life Admetus' wife, Alcestis. Heracles, of course, was famous for abducting Cerberus, the guard dog from the Underworld, and in his rescue of Alcestis Heracles fought Thanatos, Death himself. In his *Andromache* Euripides has Hermione, daughter of Helen of Troy, accuse the heroine of causing her to miscarry through *pharmaka*. The nurse in Euripides Phaedra recommends a *philtron*, which will 'neither shame nor derange', to cure Phaedra's illicit love for Hippolytus, her stepson.

Sosiphanes of Syracuse, another tragic poet, asserts that the association between Thessaly and witchcraft is so strong that not only witches but all Thessalian girls can draw down the moon.

Menander's lost plays entitled *Deisidaemon* and *Theophoroumenos* both included magic. Pliny the Elder reports that Menander's *Thessala* featured the witches of infamously magical Thessaly. Donatus (on Terence's *Eunuchus* 9.3) mentions Menander's lost *Phasma*, *The Ghost*, in which a stepson sees his stepmother's beautiful daughter and thinks he has seen a ghost.

These references indicate very clearly that purveyors of black magic were a feature of everyday Greek life: their presence, if not their actions and intentions, was an accepted fact.

42. THE PRE-SOCRATICS WERE RATIONAL; THEY ASKED SEARCHING QUESTIONS LIKE 'WHERE DOES EVERYTHING COME FROM?'

Greek philosophy has its roots in what we today call the natural sciences; indeed, we ourselves called the study of nature natural philosophy until the end of the nineteenth century. The pre-Socratics were rational; they asked searching questions like where does everything come from? What is everything created from? How do we explain the plurality of things in nature? How do we describe nature mathematically?

Thales of Miletus (*c.* 624–*c.* 546 BC) is our first philosopher; he was also an astronomer and mathematician and the first scientist to explain natural phenomena without recourse to mythology or the supernatural. According to Aristotle, Thales taught that the fundamental principle of nature (the *arche*) was water and that everything comes from water. He was also the first to define general principles and develop hypotheses. Controversy surrounds the assertion that Thales predicted a solar eclipse (which did take place during his lifetime), but what is more certain is that Thales made many crucial mathematical discoveries – not least that the circle is bisected by its diameter and that a triangle inscribed in a semicircle is always a right-angled triangle – Thales' theorem.

Anaximander (610–546 BC) was the first writer on philosophy with *On the Nature of Things*. His first principle was a nebulous, limitless and infinite substance (*apeiron*), from which the opposites, hot and cold, moist and dry, came. This all created earth, sea and sky enveloped by wheels of fire from which emanated the sun, moon and stars. The opposites were also responsible for meteorological events and the origins of animal life. His earth was a flat disc; human life originated from embryos floating in the sea. He was the first man to make a map of the known world. Anaximenes (585–525 BC) took for his principle (*aer*) air modified by condensation and rarefaction into fire, wind, clouds, water, stones and earth. Pythagoras of Samos (582–496 BC) saw the world in perfect harmony totally dependent on number; he aimed at encouraging mankind to lead a harmonious life. His famous eponymous theorem endures today but his work on the octave and basic harmonies is just as significant. Heraclitus of Ephesus (535–475 BC) believed that all things in nature are in a state of perpetual flux (*panta rhei*), connected by logical pattern, which he called *logos*. This change was essential to the cosmic order. Heraclitus taught that fire was the catalyst for this pattern and that all things originate from, and return to, fire in an eternal cyclical process.

Xenophanes of Colophon (570–470 BC) declared that the origin of things is from earth and water, with clouds formed from the sea thus accounting for celestial and meteorological phenomena. Mocking the Homeric pantheon, he believes the supreme god to be the eternal unifying force, pervading the universe, and governing it by his thought. Parmenides of Elea (510–440 BC) asserted that this one unchanging existence was the only truth and the only thing that could be conceived – multitude and change – were unreal.

43. The Atomists and their Materialistic System Was Formed by Leucippus and Democritus of Abdera

Zeno of Elea (490–430 BC) proposed four paradoxes which show that change or multiplicity is contradictory. Empedocles of Agrigentum (490–430 BC) supported the immutable nature of substance but supports too the existence of four basic forms of perceptible matter – earth, water, air, and fire – which make up the world through two ideal motive forces: love as the cause of union, and strife as the cause of separation. In addition, he asserted that perception is derived from a mechanism of pores and effluences. Anaxagoras of Clazomenae (500–428 BC) believed that divine reason (*nous*) was the crucial force.

The Atomists and their materialistic system was formed by Leucippus (fifth century BC) and Democritus of Abdera (460–370 BC). They believed that atoms – infinite in number, indivisible and imperishable, similar but distinguished by their shapes – moved eternally through the infinite void, colliding and uniting, generating objects.

Although Leucippus is usually credited with inventing atomism, Strabo asserts that Greek atomism can be traced back to Moschus of Sidon, who lived at the time of the Trojan wars. This was given credence in the seventeenth century when Henry More traced the origins of ancient atomism back, via Pythagoras and Moschus, to Moses.

The last of the pre-Socratic philosophers was Diogenes of Apollonia (born *c*. 460 BC), an eclectic philosopher who took on many principles of the Milesian school.

44. MANY MEN AND WOMEN TURNED TO AND EMBRACED THE EMERGING, ORIENTAL, MYSTERY RELIGIONS

Traditional, Olympus-based religion, with its incestuous, mythologised pantheon, became unexciting and unappealing to some; the gods appeared aloof, and offered little hope of life after death and seemed to favour the upper classes. Many men and women turned to and embraced the emerging, oriental, mystery religions. These cults originated from the exotic east and were predicated on the land and fertility, on birth and rebirth. To outsiders they were obscure and arcane; however, they were much more personal and participation was exclusive to initiates, like-minded people. Their eschatologies often enshrined birth and rebirth, and as such they offered hope of life after death, immortality.

The word mystery comes from Greek *mysteria* (μυστήρια), meaning 'secret rite or doctrine'. An initiate was a *mystes*, 'one who has been initiated', from *myein*, to close, a reference to secrecy through keeping your eyes and mouth shut.

By definition, it is difficult to say very much about any of the mysteries because they were, of course, mysterious, and very little was written down about them. However, the most famous were the Eleusinian Mysteries based on the myth of Demeter and Persephone, whose abduction and incarceration in Hades led to the four seasons and the fecundity of the earth. Participation was exclusive to priests and priestesses, initiates experiencing the ceremony for the first time, others who had participated at least once before, and those who had attained *épopteia* (ἐποπτεία) or contemplation, who had learned the secrets of the mysteries of Demeter.

The Dionysian Mysteries, after Dionysus, made great use of intoxicants (drugs and alcohol) and other trance-inducing activities like dance and music to shake off inhibitions and social constraints, liberating the individual initiate, which significantly included those marginalized by Greek society: women, slaves and foreigners. In time, these mysteries moved from the chthonic to more of a transcendental, mystical experience.

The female initiate played the role of Ariadne, Dionysus' bride in the underworld. The ritual symbol of Dionysus was originally a goat's penis, and later a fig-wood phallus. The initiate then took part in a wedding feast where flagellation was endured and possibly ritualised hangings. For men, initiation was rather more straightforward and somewhat less erotic. It involved a descent into the underworld, or *katabasis*, performed in caves, catacombs or temples. The descent was satirised in Aristophanes' *The Frogs* (405 BC). After this, the initiate communed with Dionysus through wine and was then known as a Bacchus, shown the secret contents of the *liknon* (a simple agricultural implement) and presented with the *thyrsos* wand – staff of giant fennel covered with ivy vines and leaves, and topped with a pine cone.

Herodotus and Euripides tell of Bacchic-Orphic beliefs and practices: itinerant religion specialists and purveyors of secret knowledge, called Orpheotelestai, performed the *teletai*, private rites for the remission of sins. As with the Pythagoreans, the Orphics were vegetarians and could not be buried in woollen garments.

45. Herodotus Cannot Resist Involving Magic to Add Spice to His Anecdotes

Herodotus cannot resist involving magic to add spice to his anecdotes. He describes the magical powers enjoyed by Aristeas of Proconnesus, who lived 100 years previously in the sixth century BC. One day Aristeas apparently dropped down dead while in a local fullers. The news of his death was disputed by a traveller who claimed that he had just seen Aristeas on the road to Cyzicus.

Indeed, Aristeas' relatives could find no trace of him when they searched the fullers; he did, however, show up seven years later and composed his *Arimaspeia*, a poem of travels in faraway lands among fantastical creatures. After that he disappeared again, and 240 years later he turned up in the city of Metapontum as a *phasma* (a ghost in the shape of a crow), and instructed the locals to build an altar and a statue in honour of Apollo. The oracle at Delphi verified the story, fascinating in its combination of bilocation, metempsychosis and reanimation, and rematerialization.

Herodotus also gives us an account of Melissa's *nekuomanteion* and Periander's necrophilia. Melissa is reticent at first because the clothes in which she was buried had not been burned and she was as cold as hell in hell. Periander had thrown his loaves into a cold oven, as it were, indicating that he had had sex with Melissa's corpse. He also tells the story of Salmoxis and the Getae. These Thracians believed themselves to be immortal and, instead of dying, went to the demon Salmoxis, a former slave of Pythagoras who got rich after his emancipation and set up a kind of salon for local dignitaries. Anyone dining with Salmoxis then became immortal and lived in an Elysian-type world; Salmoxis himself inhabited an underground room for three years in what is a semi-*katabasis*.

Herodotus also gives us a picture of the Persian magi and their practices. While encamped outside Troy on his way to invade Greece, Xerxes sacrificed 1,000 oxen to Athene with the help of the magi. The Persian sacrifice to a Greek goddess did not help his cause – the terrified soldiers of Xerxes' thought that the magi were raising the ghosts of the Trojan army, who were buried thereabouts after the Trojan War. On crossing the River Strymon the Persians sacrificed white horses and buried alive nine local boys and girls. To quell a three-day storm, the magi sacrificed to the dead and sang incantations. In describing obscure Persian-magic users called the Neuri, Herodotus reports that they were *goetes* (sorcerers) and that they transmogrified into wolves for a few days each year – thus forging a link between sorcerers and werewolves.

The leading historian of a generation later – Thucydides – has little patience with conjurers or the supernatural. However, these magic users affected the lives of the people he describes, so he is forced to raise the matter, even if obliquely; for example, he refers to the ghost of Pausanias and the evocators who summoned it.

46. Cleisthenes Abolished Patronymics and Replaced Them with Demonymics

Cleisthenes (b. *c.* 570 BC) finished what Solon started in relation to the establishment of Athenian democracy. His first significant action was the overthrow of Hippias, the tyrant son of Peistratus, with help of the Alcmaeonidae, Cleisthenes' Athenian tribe. This left Isagoras, archon in 508, and Cleisthenes' rivals, but Isagoras won the day when he gained the support of the Spartan king Cleomenes I and expelled Cleisthenes. This was effected on the pretext of the Alcmaeonid curse.

Megacles was the first notable Alcmaeonid. He murdered the followers of Cylon of Athens during the attempted coup of 632 BC – Cylon had taken sanctuary at the temple of Athena. Megacles and his Alcmaeonid followers were then the subject of an eternal curse and exiled from the city. Even the bodies of buried Alcmaeonidae were dug up and removed from the city. The Alcmaeonidae were henceforth debarred from ruling in Athens but they were allowed back into the city in 594 BC, during the archonship of Solon.

Cleisthenes left Athens an exile, and Isagoras ruled unopposed. He repossessed hundreds of Athenians' homes, exiling them on the pretext that they too were cursed. He tried to dissolve Solon's *boule* (βουλή) but the council resisted, and when the Athenians declared their support for the council, Isagoras and his supporters fled to the Acropolis and were besieged there for two days. On day three they fled the city and were banished. Cleisthenes was recalled with hundreds of exiles, and took control of Athens.

Reforms began in earnest. To prevent further internecine strife between the tribes, which had led to the tyranny, he increased the four traditional tribes based on family relations to ten tribes formed according to their residence (*deme*). Cleisthenes abolished patronymics in favour of demonymics – a name given according to the one's *deme*, to inculcate a sense of belonging to a *deme*. He established sortation: the random selection of citizens to fill government positions as opposed to it being based on kinship or heredity. He reorganized the *boule*, increasing membership to 500 members (fifty from each tribe) and introduced the bouletic oath, 'To advise according to the laws what was best for the people.' The court system (*dikasteria*) was overhauled so that it could call on between 201 and 5,001 jurors each day, up to 500 from each tribe. The *boule* proposed laws to the assembly of voters, who met in Athens around forty times a year for this purpose. Bills could be rejected, passed or returned for amendments by the assembly.

Cleisthenes introduced ostracism, first used in 487 BC, whereby a vote from over 6,000 citizens would exile a citizen for ten years, particularly those thought to pose a threat to democracy. The word comes from the *ostraka* cast in the voting process – free and readily available pottery shards that served as scrap paper, as opposed to papyrus imported from Egypt as high-quality and expensive writing material.

Cleisthenes called his reforms *isonomia*: 'equality in the eyes of the law'. Whatever the name, Athens was now being run by the Athenians.

47. The Persians Posed the First Real External Threat to the City-States of Ancient Greece

Cyrus the Great was the founder of the Achaemenid Empire. He built his empire by conquering the Median Empire, then the Lydian Empire and eventually the Neo-Babylonian Empire. He led an expedition into central Asia, which resulted in major campaigns that were described by Herodotus as having brought 'into subjection every nation without exception'. Cyrus the Great is remembered for his good work in human rights, politics, and military strategy, and a general influence on both Eastern and Western civilizations, leaving his stamp on the national identity of modern Iran. Achaemenid influence also extended as far as Athens, where many Athenians adopted Achaemenid Persian culture as their own, in a reciprocal cultural exchange.

It was the Persians who posed the first real external threat to the city-states of ancient Greece. The Persian Wars were a series of conflicts between the Achaemenid Empire of Persia and Greek city-states. They started in 499 BC and continued until 449 BC. Trouble started as far back as 547 BC when the Persians under Cyrus conquered Greek Ionia. The Persians installed tyrants to rule each of the Ionian city-states. In 499 BC, Aristagoras, the tyrant of Miletus, set out to conquer the island of Naxos, with Persian support. It was a complete disaster, and seeing the inevitable, Aristagoras incited all of Hellenic Asia Minor into rebellion against the Persians – the beginning of the Ionian Revolt, which lasted until 493 BC, sucking in more and more regions of Asia Minor.

Aristagoras obtained the support of Athens and Eretria, who in 498 BC captured and razed Sardis, the Persian regional capital. The Persian king Darius the Great vowed revenge on Athens and Eretria and so the revolt went on, the two sides in stalemate from 497 to 495 BC. In 494 BC, the Persians regrouped and launched an attack on Miletus, the epicentre of the revolt. At the Battle of Lade, the Ionians suffered a decisive defeat, and the rebellion collapsed. With the last remaining rebels extinguished in 493, Aristagoras secured military support from Athens and Eretria, and in 498 BC these forces helped to capture and burn the Persian regional capital of Sardis. Darius vowed to have revenge on Athens and Eretria for this act.

Darius had not forgotten Sardis; how could he? Herodotus tells us that after Sardis Darius took his bow and shot an arrow into the sky and said: 'Zeus, allow me to take vengeance on the Athenians!' At the same time he ordered one of his servants to say to him every day before dinner, three times: 'Master, remember the Athenians.' And so it was in 492 BC that the first Persian invasion of Greece was launched. Mardonius took Thrace and Macedon before the campaign came to a premature end. In 490 BC a second force came across the Aegean under the command of Datis and Artaphernes and subjugated the Cyclades, before besieging, taking and razing Eretria. Athens was next.

48. THE BATTLE OF MARATHON GAVE PROOF THAT THE MIGHTY PERSIANS COULD BE DEFEATED

One of the long-term effects of the decisive battle of Marathon was that it enabled Athens to believe in its ability to defend itself and to see a long-term political and military future. The Athenians proved that the mighty Persians could be defeated and that organised resistance was well worthwhile. For that reason, the battle has been called 'a defining moment in the development of European culture'.

In September 490 BC the Persians arrived in numbers having taken Eretria. An invasion force of around 20,000 infantry and cavalry poured from a Persian armada of 600 triremes north of Athens. This was the revenge that Darius has promised. Valuable intelligence was gained from the exiled and disaffected Athenian tyrant Hippias.

In response, Athens mobilized 10,000 hoplites: the two armies clashed on the Plain of Marathon, 26 miles north of Athens – a site favourable to the Persian cavalry, surrounded as it was by hills and sea. The Athenians were bolstered by 1,000 troops from Plataea. The Persian force was again commanded by Datis and Artaphernes. Surveying the scene, the Greeks had pause for thought. They sought help from the Spartans by sending a runner, the famous Pheidippides, the 140 miles, which he easily covered, arriving the next day. The Spartans, however, were detained by a religious festival which they could not leave until after the next full moon. The Spartans eventually showed up but by then it was all over.

One of the Greek generals – Miltiades – passionately, and successfully, urged his men not to hesitate and do battle. He commanded the Greek hoplites to form a line equal in length to that of the Persians. Then, in an act of apparent tactical madness, because he lacked supporting cavalry and archers, Miltiades ordered his men to attack the Persian line. Predictably, the centre of the Greek line collapsed in the chaos, but the flanks engulfed and slaughtered the Persians. Around 6,400 Persians died that day to Greek losses of 192. This is how Herodotus described it: 'The Athenians ... charged the barbarians at a run. Now the distance between the two armies was little short of eight furlongs [approximately a mile] The Persians, therefore, when they saw the Greeks coming on at speed, made ready to receive them, although it seemed to them that the Athenians were bereft of their senses, and bent upon their own destruction; for they saw a mere handful of men coming on at a run without either horsemen or archers.'

Defeat at Marathon would have meant total defeat for Athens, since the Athenian army mustered at Marathon was the only Athenian army there was. It was imperative, therefore, that they keep the Persian army pinned down at Marathon, blocking both exits from the plain, and preventing the Persians from attacking Athens. The surviving Persians escaped to try an assault on what they thought was an undefended Athens. The Greeks, however, made a forced march back to Athens and repelled the Persians.

49. Pheidippides Takes News to Athens Regarding the Outcome of the Battle

Given that the battle was so pivotal in the future of Athens and ancient Greece in general, it is hardly surprising that a number of legends grew up around the Battle of Marathon. The most famous concerns the runner Pheidippides who took news to Athens regarding the outcome of the battle. We have already met him running the 280-mile round trip from Marathon to Sparta – disappointed, no doubt, to discover that the Spartans had other priorities. After the battle he may have had to join the rapid, armour-encumbered march back to Athens to head off the Persians.

Herodotus adds that Pheidippides was paid a visit by Pan en route to Sparta and was asked why the Athenians did not honour him. An awestruck Pheidippides spluttered that that would all change and that the Athenians would honour him from then on. The god was happy with this promise and appeared in the Battle of Marathon to inflict on the Persians the irrational fear that bore his name: 'panic'. After the battle, a sacred precinct was established for Pan on the north slope of the Acropolis, and a sacrifice was offered every year.

The victory won similar favour for Artemis Agrotera (Artemis the Huntress) after a vow made by Athens before the conflict to sacrifice a number of goats equal to the number of Persians slain. So great was the number (6,400) that the decision had to be made to offer 500 goats a year until the number was fulfilled. Xenophon records that in his day, some ninety years after the battle, goats were still being slaughtered in sacrifice.

Plutarch tells us that the Athenians saw the ghost of King Theseus, mythical hero of Athens, leading the army in full battle regalia in the charge against the Persians.

Pausanias adds that: 'They say too that there chanced to be present in the battle a man of rustic appearance and dress. Having slaughtered many of the foreigners with a plough he was seen no more after the engagement. When the Athenians made enquiries at the oracle, the god merely ordered them to honour Echetlaeus ("he of the Plough-tail") as a hero.'

The most famous legend has Pheidippides running from Marathon to Athens after the battle, to announce the jubilant Greek victory with νενικήκαμεν; 'we've won!' Job done, he fell down dead from exhaustion. The story is first published in Plutarch's *On the Glory of Athens*, who quotes from Heracleides of Pontus, giving the runner's name as either Thersipus of Erchius or Eucles. It was Lucian who gave us the name Philippides (not Pheidippides).

The feat – real or otherwise – was adopted in 1896 by the creators of the modern Olympic Games as the marathon event, based on the legendary version of events, with the competitors running from Marathon to Athens. The distance eventually became fixed at 26 miles 385 yards, the approximate distance from Marathon to Athens.

50. Purveyors of Black Magic Were a Feature of Everyday Greek Life

Plato is anti-magic, but he takes the subject seriously. He expatiates on ghosts and their tendency to frequent graves; on the immortality of the soul (*Phaedo*); the nature of death, judgement of the dead (*Gorgias*), Orphism *(Cratylus)* and metempsychosis (*Phaedrus*). His *Myth of Er* describes Er's experience in the underworld. In the *Laws* he recommends the death penalty for anyone harming or killing through the use of magical dolls (*kolossoi*), spells, charms and incantations. Also, in the *Republic* he vilifies beggar-priests and prophets (*manteis*) with their sacrifices and incantations. In the *Georgias*, Plato also tells that the Thessalian witches, who draw down the moon, cannot do it with impunity.

The story of Gyges illustrates the magical power of some rings: Gyges finds a ring and soon realises that a simple manipulation can render him invisible; he uses this new power to seduce the king of Lydia's wife, to depose the king with her help and assume the crown.

In the fourth century BC Aristotle records Pythagoras' association two centuries before with Pherecydes of Syros, a peripatetic miracle man and one of the first proponents of metempsychosis (when the soul finds a new body). He also tells us how Pythagoras announced to waiting locals in Metapontum eager to get their hands on a ship's cargo that the pilot was a corpse; how he killed a poisonous snake in Etruria by biting it – snake blasting; how a river greeted him with 'Hail, Pythagoras' as he crossed it; and how he turned up in the cities of Croton and Metapontum both at the same time – an instance of bilocation. Aristotle maintains that Pythagoras had a golden thigh.

In the third century AD, Porphyry corroborates much of this in his *Life of Pythagoras,* adding that Pythagoras could predict earthquakes, end pestilence, and calm storms, seas and rivers. Empedocles, Epimenides and Abaris had similar magical gifts, the last travelling through the air on an arrow – a kind of broomstick. Aristotle also provides a valuable disquisition on the aphrodisiacal *hippomanes* in the *History of Animals.* Clearchus of Soli, a pupil of Aristotle, describes how a special soul-drawing wand, the *psuchoulkos rhabdos,* can draw the soul of a young boy out of his body, and then replace it intact.

One of Theophrastus' characters is Deisidaemon, who comes over as suffering from a kind of obsessive compulsive disorder manifesting as 'an obsessive fear of the gods, a penchant for adoration and cultic performance, superstitious awe of portents both in daily life and in dreams, and the concomitant inclination to ward off or prevent possible mishaps by magical or ritual acts, especially through continuous purifications'. This sketch lends support to the belief that such superstitious paranoid characters were alive and well in Athenian society. Theophrastus would have seen them, met them and would have based his sketches as much on such encounters as from watching the plays of his contemporary playwright Menander, another rich source of such characters.

51. THE HOPLITE AND PHALANX WERE THE DEFINING CHARACTERISTICS OF THE ATHENIAN ARMY

The Athenian army at the time of Marathon had evolved with the evolution of the *polis*. The hoplite and phalanx were the defining characteristics: hoplites, the citizen-soldiers of the *polis*, were infantry in armour, armed with a 6-ft-long spear and a bronze-faced wooden round shield (*hoplon* or *aspis*). The phalanx was a formation of these troops with the ability to advance with shields locked together and spears pointed forward. A back-up weapon was the *xiphos*, a short sword for emergency use when the spear was broken or mislaid in battle. Armour comprised a helmet, metal greaves and a breastplate made of bronze, leather, or thick cloth. In terms of equipment, the hoplite was much better fitted out than his Persian counterpart. The hoplite was probably established by 650 BC lasting until the end of the third century BC. Generally speaking every man had to serve at least two years in the army.

For every hoplite there was an attendant: a lightly armed man, either a poor citizen or a trusted slave. These attendants carried the hoplite's *aspis* before the battle, and the baggage. They were usually armed with javelins, spears, slings or bows. If needed they acted as skirmishers before the main battle, and guarded the camp while the fighting was going on.

The phalanx – a close, tight formation – was usually eight ranks deep but sometimes as few as four. The number of ranks went up over time and at the battle of Leuctra in 371 BC, there were fifty rows in the Boetian phalanx.

Early raids to steal cattle or grab lands gradually gave way to clashes between *poleis*, but even these were of a transitory nature as soldiers then had pressing day jobs (many as farmers) that they needed to get back to and cultivate in order to earn money and to pay for their expensive armour and weaponry. Early Greek warfare, then, was restricted by the distance an army could travel, by the season (winter was not an option) and by scale. No *polis* could sustain heavy casualties or long campaigns, so one-off set-piece battles were the order of the day. That is until the formidable Persians came and the Athenians probably surprised themselves with the ease of their victory at Marathon.

Initially interstate hoplite battles were short, uncomplicated and brutal. Pushing and shoving were key functions in what was a notably poor formation in terms of manoeuverability, with little opportunity to pursue a fleeing enemy. Casualties tended to be low at 5 per cent of defeated combatants and victory was sealed by ransoming back prisoners of war in a process called 'Custom of the Dead Greeks'.

Sometimes Greek armies included light infantry, with javelin throwers, peltasts (from the word for a Thracian light shield), and cavalry deployed as scouts or to repel skirmishers. However, horses were very expensive so cavalry was open only to nobles and the rich. Some city-states also employed tactics using slingers and archers.

52. XERXES AMASSED THE LARGEST AND MOST WELL-EQUIPPED FIGHTING FORCE EVER PUT INTO THE FIELD

Xerxes was the fourth king of the Achaemenid Empire. He ruled from 486 BC until his assassination in 465 BC at the hands of Artabanus, the commander of the royal bodyguard. It was predicted that Xerxes, one of the oldest of Darius' eleven sons, would succeed his father. The official title of Xerxes I was 'Shahanshah', which means 'king of kings'. He turns up as the Ahasuerus of Persia in the *Book of Esther*. Xerxes is best known for the huge expedition he mounted against Greece in 480 BC, which, according to Herodotus, was the largest and most well-equipped fighting force ever put into the field. His father Darius died before he could retaliate after Marathon and win his vengeance for Sardis. It fell, therefore, to Xerxes to carry out his father's threats, and so he amassed this huge army.

First, in 485, he dealt with insurrection in Babylon and revolution in Egypt. The former was an ally of Cyrus and of Darius but Xerxes showed his indifference to old ties and an arrogant, cavalier attitude to religious and diplomatic protocol and respect when he melted down the highly prestigious golden statue of Marduk, the patron deity of Babylon. Xerxes spent four years building up his forces but the omens, in the form of an eclipse, were not good. Xerxes, displaying yet more hubris, chose to ignore it, but Pythias, a Lydian ally, saw it as an omen of impending doom and had the temerity to ask Xerxes if his eldest son could be discharged from the army to look after him in his old age and become his heir. Xerxes saw this as a question mark over his chances of success and, incandescent, chopped this son in half, placed the two carcasses on either side of the road, and marched his troops off between them.

According to Herodotus, the size of the Xerxes expedition was an eye-watering 2 million men and 4,000 ships. A more sober assessment puts the troop numbers at 100,000 and 1,207 triremes. In order to effect free passage of his navy, he had a canal dug across the Isthmus of Actium near Mount Athos, the remains of which can still be seen today. Xerxes stood on the threshold of Europe, ready to cross the Hellespont, when, as Herodotus writes, he became emotional and existential. The sight of his forces 'first gave Xerxes a feeling of deep self-satisfaction, but later he began to weep. When his uncle, Artabanus … noticed that Xerxes was crying he said, "My lord, a short while ago you were feeling happy with your situation and now you are weeping. What a total change of mood!" "Yes," Xerxes answered. "I was reflecting on things and it occurred to me how short the sum total of human life is, which made me feel compassion. Look at all these people – but not one of them will still be alive in a hundred years' time."' (VII.45-46).

53. Xerxes Ordered His Men to Give the Hellespont Three Hundred Lashes

Persian preparations continued apace: tons of materiel and food supplies were stored up, the canal was dug at Chalkidike, and boat bridges were built across the Hellespont. Even the oracle at Delphi gloomily advised the Athenians to 'fly to the world's end'. What, in effect, Xerxes was doing was marching over the sea and sailing over the land.

The omens, or the weather, continued to disappoint the Persians too. But the Hellespont had to be bridged. Herodotus describes it best in an episode of Xerxes' madness reminiscent, in its absurd personalization of the megalomania and cruelty displayed, of Caligula nearly 500 years later: 'The Phoenicians and the Egyptians ... had just finished bridging the straits when a violent storm erupted which completely smashed and destroyed everything. This news made Xerxes furious. He ordered his men to give the Hellespont three hundred lashes and to sink a pair of shackles into the sea. I once heard that they also dispatched men to brand the Hellespont as well. Be that as it may, he did tell the men thrashing the sea to revile it in terms you would never hear from a Greek. "Bitter water, they said, this is your punishment for wronging your master when he did no wrong to you. King Xerxes will cross you, with or without your consent. People are right not to sacrifice to a muddy, brackish stream like you!" So the sea was punished at his orders and he had the supervisors of the bridging of the Hellespont beheaded.' (VII.34-36).

54. THE PERSIANS SACK ATHENS

The Greeks in 480 reacted by despatching a force of 10,000 hoplites to hold the valley of Tempē, but the city-states concerned were hesitant and their support was lukewarm. In the end they had second thoughts and withdrew when they saw the massive army facing them. Nevertheless they regrouped and, despite mutual suspicion, formed a joint army of between 6,000 and 7,000 men. Interestingly, the 300 Spartans recruited were all men who had living sons; Leonidas was anxious that the war did not exterminate any Spartan families.

The Greeks were posted to defend the pass at Thermopylae 95 miles north of Athens, the last place from which Artemision could be defended – the Persians had to go through the pass to enter mainland Greece.

A total of 80,000 Persian troops, including the crack force the Immortals, approached Thermopylae (the Pass of the Hot Springs), where Xerxes invited the Greeks to surrender. Their commander, Leonidas, retorted by inviting Xerxes to *'molōn labe'* ('come and get us'). The battle began. The Spartans held out on the first day of savage close-quarter fighting, feigning a chaotic retreat. The second day was much the same until, that is, Ephialtes, a local shepherd from Trachis, told the Persians about an alternative route – the Anopaia path – which would allow them to attack the Greek southern flank. Leonidas ordered the Greek forces to withdraw.

On the third day of the battle Leonidas rallied his small force – the survivors from the original Spartan 300, 700 Thespians and 400 Thebans – and began a rearguard action to defend the pass to the last man and to delay the Persians and allow the rest of the Greek force to retreat or await relief from a larger Greek force. Leonidas was killed, as were the rest of the Greeks. After the battle,

Xerxes ordered that Leonidas' head be stuck on a stake and displayed at the battlefield. Leonidas, then, was that king of Sparta whom the oracle predicted must die.

Before Artemision, the exposed Persian fleet lost 400 triremes in a devastating storm off the coast of Magnesia and 200 more in a second tempest off Euboea. When the two fleets clashed, the battle was indecisive and when they learnt of Thermopylae, the Greek navy withdrew to Salamis. The Persians went on to sack an evacuated Athens.

Like Marathon, the battle at Thermopylae has been 'sadly contaminated with sentimental journalism' according to one historian. Its strategic significance was that it allowed the Greeks to go on to fight at Artemision where the Persian fleet suffered significant loss – factors which ultimately dictated the result of the war. Indecisive as it was, it gave the young Athenian fleet invaluable battle experience, and intelligence regarding the much more experienced Persian navy. The engagement and the devastating losses caused by the storms reduced the opposition numbers considerably, making the Persian fleet potentially a much more assailable foe at Salamis.

55. Circe is the First 'Classical' Witch

Witches were part of the fabric of ancient Greek life. A witch was usually totally unscrupulous, devoid of any morals, and prepared to do whatever it took to get her way. They were often liminal people at the margins of society – peripatetic and rootless. In mythology, they are magical, evil and scheming; in literature witches are excoriated and ridiculed. Circe, Medea and their goddess Hecate never existed of course, but they are indicative of what sorceresses did in the real world. Generations of Greeks from the time of Homer would have heard or read about them.

Multi-potion, *polypharmakos,* Circe is the first 'classical' witch, a witchy kind of woman who provides a template for witchery. In her encounter with Odysseus, she displays and implements all the qualities any witch should perfect: magic – sympathetic and otherwise; invocations – curses and sacrifices; necromancy – that gold standard of invocations; *pharmaka* – more magic, poisons, love philtres and aphrodisiacs, potions that restore youth or are form-changing.

Circe, in Homer's *Odyssey,* unhelpfully changes Odysseus' crew into pigs (and back again), at the wave of a staff and with a single spell and a simple potion. She is anxious, no doubt, to keep a ready supply of men available to satisfy her lust. Odysseus himself is immune from this form-changing because Mercury, in his role as a male sorcerer, had given him *molu*, a kind of snowdrop with protective and mystical properties. Immune from the porcine magic as he is, Odysseus nevertheless succumbs to Circe's abundant physical charms and the two enter on a torrid affair, during which she reveals his future, including Odysseus' forthcoming appointment with dead people in his necromancy.

Circe is a skilful spell-maker and she uses potions to good effect – the perfect example of the triadic association between drugs, spells and medicine which prevailed in the ancient world. She has other traditional witchy attributes: she can render herself invisible, she can fly through the air and she has the power to emasculate her lovers. After a refreshing bath Odysseus convinces Circe that his men need to be restored to their previous form. This she does, with the added bonus that they each re-emerge rejuvenated: 'younger than they were before, and much taller and better looking'.

Elsewhere Circe is also a necromancer, purifying Jason and Medea after the murder of Apsyrtus and helping to lay his ghost; she calls up ghosts before she changes Pircus's comrades into animals – more form-changing magic. Odysseus is raised from the dead by Circe after he was killed by Telegonus. Manto, the daughter of the seer Tiresias, is compared to Circe and Medea, but without the evil bits, showing that some witches could be a force for the good, and not always malevolent.

Circe embodies everything a witch needs to practice effectively: magical skill and magical accoutrements, mystical plants, erotic magic, rejuvenation skills, and a working knowledge of eschatology. All of these facets, in the next five to six hundred years, were cultivated and developed in the Greek world.

56. HERODOTUS WAS A 'BARBARIAN LOVER'

Herodotus's approach was new in Western literature and his *Histories* in general account for the claim that he invented history. In his *Persian Fire*, Tom Holland puts it well: 'For the first time, a chronicler set himself to trace the origins of a conflict not to a past so remote so as to be utterly fabulous, nor to the whims and wishes of some god, nor to a people's claim to manifest destiny, but rather explanations he could verify personally.'

Thucydides offers a backhanded compliment when he starts his history beyond the point where Herodotus left off at the Siege of Sestos in 479 BC, suggesting that the former's account needed no revision. Much later, Plutarch (*c.* AD 46–AD 120), however, was less sanguine. In his *On the Malignity of Herodotus*, he describes Herodotus as '*Philobarbaros*' (barbarian-lover), and criticises him for not being sufficiently pro-Greek.

Herodotus gives us his aims and scope, his unique selling point, in writing the *Histories* (literally *Enquiries*, from ἱστορία): 'Here are presented the results of the enquiry carried out by Herodotus of Halicarnassus. The purpose is to prevent the traces of human events from being erased by time, and to preserve the fame of the important and remarkable achievements produced by both Greeks and non-Greeks; among the matters covered is, in particular, the cause of the hostilities between Greeks and non-Greeks.' And in doing so, provides a template for all successive history writing to this day.

Facts apart, his history is peppered with stories, dubious tales and fantasy. He described a hippopotamus, for example – something he probably never saw himself, but was very illuminating to his fellow Greeks, most of whom would also would not have seen one: 'The hippopotamus is held sacred in the district of Papremis, but not elsewhere.

This animal has four legs, cloven hoofs like an ox, a snub nose, a horse's mane and tail, conspicuous tusks, a voice like a horse's neigh, and is about the size of a very large ox. Its hide is so thick and tough that when dried it can be made into spear-shafts.'

Truly monstrous ants: 'There is found in this desert a kind of ant of great size - bigger than a fox, though not so big as a dog.' He also described strange Egyptians: 'the women go to market and men stay at home and weave [the exact opposite to Greek practice]. Women even urinate standing up and men sitting down.

Pheros was a King of Egypt who went blind. After 10 years the oracle at Buto said he had served his punishment and would be cured if he washed his eyes out with the urine of a woman who had never slept with any man except her husband. So he tried his wife's urine ... it didn't work, then many other women until one worked and he could see again. All those women whose urine failed were collected together and burned. He then married the lady whose urine worked.'

57. The Battle of Salamis Rendered the Greek Mainland More or Less Safe from the Persians

According to Aeschylus, the Greek fleet numbered 310 triremes – and he should know, he was there. According to Herodotus, the Persian fleet numbered 1,207 triremes. Time was not on Xerxes' side: he had planned to conclude the conquest of Greece in one campaign. Moreover, his huge force could not be provisioned forever and he presumably did not want to be away from the centre of his empire for much longer. Thermopylae demonstrated that a frontal assault against the Greeks was pointless; and the allies were entrenched across the Isthmus, thus precluding the chances of subduing the rest of Greece by land. However, Thermopylae also showed that the Greeks could be outflanked and destroyed. The Persian navy could effect this and destroy the allied navy, thus forcing the Greeks to surrender. On the other hand, Themistocles, in charge of the allied fleet, believed that by sinking the Persian fleet, he could scupper the Persian threat.

Moreover, Herodotus observes that Queen Artemisia of Caria had a more objective and considered view of the situation. She pointed out to Xerxes that fighting a sea battle was unnecessary: 'If you do not hurry to fight at sea, but keep your ships here and stay near land, or even advance into the Peloponnese, then, my lord, you will easily accomplish what you had in mind in coming here. The Hellenes are not able to hold out against you for a long time, but you will scatter them, and they will each flee to their own cities.'

Be that as it may, Xerxes needed to evict the Greeks from Salamis so that he could use the port of Phaleron to supply his army. Herodotus tells us that Themistocles ordered a slave to row ashore and tell the Persians that the Greeks were abandoning their position so the Persians would easily defeat the Greeks. Under cover of darkness the Persians entered the narrow strait only to be attacked on their flank. A pro-Persian Egyptian squadron tried to block the Greek retreat to the north, but it was defeated by allied Corinthian ships. At least one third of the Persian vessels were destroyed.

Xerxes witnessed this shambles, sitting arrogantly on Mount Aigaleos on his specially erected throne. Some shipwrecked Phoenicians put the defeat down to the cowardly Ionians; Xerxes had the Phoenicians beheaded for slandering 'nobler men'. The rest of the Phoenicians sailed home.

Salamis rendered the Greek mainland more or less safe from subjugation. Xerxes abandoned Attica, leaving his general, Mardonius, to finish the job, wintering in Boeotia and Thessaly. The Athenians went back to their burnt-out city but the following year, 479 BC, Mardonius retook Athens with the allied army still guarding the Isthmus. The allies, led by the Spartans, confronted Mardonius near the city of Plataea.

58. Aeschylus Wrote Seventy or so Plays

The father of Greek drama, a mere seven of his estimated seventy or so plays have survived. As we have seen, Aeschylus was a witness to the Battle of Salamis (and indeed Marathon too), and so great was the significance of war in the ancient Greek world that Aeschylus' epitaph celebrates his participation at Marathon but makes no mention of his phenomenal ability and success as a playwright. Aristotle notes that he increased the number of characters in his plays to inject conflict and interaction between them – previously actors had interacted only with the chorus. As far as we know, he was the first to produce plays in a trilogy; the *Oresteia* is the only extant example of the form from antiquity.

It is worth quoting his graphic and passionate description of Salamis as given in his tragedy the *Persae*, if only because it is a highly unusual setting for a real-world battle description. *The Persians* is the only surviving classical Greek tragedy to deal with a contemporary event – and a useful source of information and detail about the Persian invasions.

> The night was passing, and the Grecian host
> By no means sought to issue forth unseen...
> Then upon all barbarians terror fell,
> Thus disappointed; for not as for flight
> The Hellenes sang the holy pæan then,
> But setting forth to battle valiantly.
> The bugle with its note inflamed them all...
> and meanwhile there was heard
> A mighty shout: "Come, O ye sons of Greeks,
> Make free your country, make your children free,
> Your wives, and fanes of your ancestral gods,
> And your sires' tombs! For all we now contend!"

And from our side the rush of Persian speech
Replied. No longer might the crisis wait.
At once ship smote on ship with brazen beak;
A vessel of the Greeks began the attack,
Crushing the stem of a Phoenician ship.
Each on a different vessel turned its prow.
At first the current of the Persian host
Withstood; but when within the strait the throng
Of ships was gathered, and they could not aid
Each other, but by their own brazen bows
Were struck, they shattered all our naval host.
The Grecian vessels not unskillfully
Were smiting round about; the hulls of ships
Were overset; the sea was hid from sight,
Covered with wreckage and the death of men;
The reefs and headlands were with corpses filled,
And in disordered flight each ship was rowed,
As many as were of the Persian host.
But they, like tunnies or some shoal of fish,
With broken oars and fragments of the wrecks
Struck us and clove us; and at once a cry
Of lamentation filled the briny sea,
Till the black darkness' eye did rescue us...
But this know well, that never in one day
Perished so great a multitude of men.

English translation from the *Persae* by Aeschylus
by William Cranston Lawton, reprinted from *Greek
Poets in English Verse* ed. William Hyde Appleton, 1893.

59. The Battles of Plataea and Mycale Formed the Climax of the Wars with Persia

Plataea and Mycale formed the climax of the wars with Persia. The victories ground out by the Greek allies finally extinguished the Persian threat to Greek control of its own homeland. The Athenians sent 8,000 hoplites, led by Aristides, along with 600 Plataean exiles to join the allied army. The Greeks, under the overall command of Pausanias, were not going to be drawn onto the plain at Plataea because it was highly favourable terrain for the Persian cavalry. Eleven days of stalemate ensued. Nevertheless, the allies attempted a retreat when the Persians breached their supply lines and Mardonius blocked off the Gargaphian Spring, the only source of water for the Greek army. The Greek line fragmented and retreated to a position near Plataea with running water available. Mardonius ordered his forces to pursue the Greeks, but the Spartans, Tegeans and Athenians halted and gave battle, routing the Persian infantry and killing Mardonius. Thebes surrendered after a short siege and the Thebans were taken away and executed. Plataea has been called 'the greatest land battle in classical Greek history'.

On the same day, the Greek fleet of 110 ships under Xanthippos of Athens attacked what remained of the Persian fleet at Mycale. They then came ashore, beat the Persian marines and burned all the Persian boats. The Ionians defected and attacked the Persians. So evaporated the Persian threat and their desire for revenge for Sardis all those years ago.

60. Orpheus and Pythagoras Were Magic Men

Given the celebrity enjoyed by Circe and Medea, it would be easy to assume that all witches were female and that the practice of witchcraft was the exclusive domain of women. Not so: a number of men flirted with and skirted round the edges of witchery, not least the early Greek philosophers. Around the fifth century BC the word *magos* started to appear, describing the Persian *mages* – trained priests with the ability to perform miracles. In time, however, as the knowledge of the *magi* reached Greece, *goes*, or sorcerer, became the word of choice. Around the same time, it seems likely that the traditional Greek's mistrust of religious nonconformity or of foreign religious practice took hold. What they did not understand or like they vilified – character assassination, particularly of women, was the standard reaction to the practitioner of strange and exotic religion.

Orpheus was held in high regard and was described as a holy man, *theios aner* – his main claim to fame was his aborted attempt to rescue Eurydice from the underworld in his famous *katabasis*. Pythagoras reputedly averted plagues and controlled the weather. Interestingly, he never attracted any of the vitriol endured by female witches down the ages. Other magical acts attributed to Pythagoras include being seen in two cities at the same time of day, a white eagle allowing him to stroke it, being greeted by a river with the words 'Hail, Pythagoras!', predicting that a dead man would be found on a ship, foreseeing the appearance of a white bear and declaring it was dead before the messenger reached him with the news, and biting a poisonous snake to death. Empedocles could heal the sick, rejuvenate the old, change the weather and summon up the dead in necromancy. For Plato, healers, sorcerers and prophets were a fact of life in Athens and had to be tolerated; they were low down in the food chain and needed to be regulated but were essentially harmless. In the *Republic* he called for magic abuse to be penalized.

Such luminaries of Greek philosophy as Pythagoras, Empedocles, Democritus and Plato went overseas to learn about magic.

61. Greek Women Were Seen and Not Heard

Thucydides said it all when he famously asserted 'The greatest glory [women can expect] is to be talked about among men as little as possible, whether in praise or blame.'

The status and rights of women may have varied from *polis* to *polis*, but, by and large, we can draw some general conclusions. We, for example, know that in Delphi, Gortyn, Thessaly, Megara and Sparta women were allowed to own land but, generally speaking, women had no legal or political status. With the coming of democracy, women, like slaves, metics and children, did not have the vote. Like slaves, they were simply part of the *oikos* (the household) under the control of the male *kyrios*: women, until they married, lived under the guardianship of their father or another male relative. On marriage the husband assumed the role of the woman's *kyrios* and would look after any legal affairs that involved her. Because their right to property was limited, Athenian women did not qualify as full citizens, as citizenship and civil and political rights were defined in relation to property. However, women could exercise some property rights through gifts, dowry or inheritance, although her *kyrios* still had the right to dispose of a woman's property as he saw fit.

Sparta, however, was another world. We have seen how women played a vital role in keeping the Spartan war machine well-oiled and efficient. Generally they enjoyed status, power, and respect unheard of in other parts of ancient Greece or in Rome. Since Spartan men were fully occupied with military training, bonding in mess life and doing battle, it fell to women to run the farms. It is estimated that by the fourth century BC,

Spartan women actually owned between 35 per cent and 40 per cent of all Spartan land and property and that by the Hellenistic Period, some of the wealthiest Spartans were women, controlling their own properties and looking after the properties of male kin who were posted away with the army.

Spartan women rarely married before the age of twenty, unlike their Athenian counterparts. Athenian women wore clothes to cover their bodies entirely and were rarely allowed to go out of the house; the clothes of the socially freer Spartan women were much looser and more revealing. Spartan girls as well as boys received an education.

Why were Athenian women so suppressed? The usual answer is that this was a throwback to ancient patriarchal society. However, it is, ironically, more to do with democracy than anything else. Athenians were obsessed with the fear that a woman might commit adultery, which would foster doubt regarding the paternity of her children and raise questions about inheritance. Crucially, if paternity could not be established, then the child could not be a citizen. Furthermore, adultery was thought to impair a woman's chastity and corrupt her mind.

One important area in which women could assert official importance and status was in religious cults, particularly cults of female deities in which they officiated as priestesses.

62. Dress Was Very Important to the Ancient Greeks

Dress was very important to the ancient Greek. The typical wardrobe comprised the *chiton, peplos, himation,* and *chlamys* with men and women alike wearing two pieces of clothing: an undergarment (*chiton* or *peplos*) and a kind of cloak (*himation* or *chlamys*). Clothes were usually homespun out of linen or wool with little cutting or sewing involved; they were held on and together with ornamental clasps or pins and a belt, or girdle (*zone*).

The *peplos* was a large rectangle of wool fabric fastened at the shoulder with a pin or brooch and with armholes on each side. The *chiton* was made of linen, long and wide, and girded around the waist. Both the *peplos* and *chiton* reached to the floor, but a man's *chiton* was knee-length or shorter. During exercise, horse riding, or manual work an *exomis* (a short *chiton*) was worn. Young men might wear a *chlamys* (short cloak) when riding. Women sometimes wore an *epiblema*, a shawl, over the *peplos* or *chiton*. For headware there was the broad-brimmed hat (*petasos*) for men.

There was little or no difference between men and women's clothing, and clothes might double up as bedding. Most clothing was undyed white, although we have evidence of decorated borders (usually purple) and vividly coloured patterns, especially for women.

Women would also wear a *strophion*, or bra, which was a wide band of wool or linen wrapped across the breasts and tied between the shoulder blades. There were hairnets (*sakkos*) and stretchy socks (*sokkoi*). Men and women might also wear triangular loincloths (*perizoma*) – women did so when menstruating. Both sexes wore leather sandals, slippers, soft shoes, or boots for outside but at home they usually went barefoot. The clothing was made either out of silk or linen but usually wool. Working the wool was, as in Rome, one of the prime responsibilities of the women of the house. For women the apparent blandness of most clothes was offset by flashy jewellery, fetching hair styles and make-up.

Early Greeks wore their hair *kome* (long), as reflected in Homer, who calls them *karekomoontes*. The fashion for Spartan boys was to have their hair cut short (*en chroi keirontes*), but when they reached puberty, they let it grow long. They took great pride in their hair, calling it the cheapest of ornaments (*kosmon adapanotatos*), and before going to battle they combed and dressed it with great care – Leonidas and his followers were caught by a Persian spy doing just that before the Battle of Thermopylae. Spartan men and women tied their hair in a knot over the crown of the head.

The Athenians were the opposite. They wore their hair long as children, and cut it off at puberty – a solemn religious act which included a libation offered to Heracles (*oinisteria*) with the hair dedicated to a river god.

In Athens the hair was fastened with golden grasshopper-shaped clasps. This fashion was called *krobylos*. Athenian women wore their hair in the same fashion (*korymbos*).

63. Sophocles Died of Sheer Happiness after Winning His Final Victory at the City Dionysia

Sophocles was the most prolific of the Greek playwrights with 120 plays to his credit. He was also the most successful with twenty or so victories out of the thirty competitions he entered; eighteen were at the City Dionysia. When he didn't win he came second, never third (last). The surviving seven plays are *Ajax, Antigone, The Women of Trachis, Oedipus the King, Electra, Philoctetes* and *Oedipus at Colonus*. Sophocles' great contribution to drama is his addition of a third actor, so reducing the importance of the chorus and enhancing character development and interaction.

The seven surviving plays apart, most of his prodigious output is in fragmentary form. Fragments of *Ichneutae* (*The Tracking Satyrs*) were found in Egypt in 1907 amounting to around half of the play, making it the best-preserved satyr play after Euripides' *Cyclops*. Fragments of the *Epigoni* set against the second siege of Thebes were discovered in April 2005.

Other fragments are from *Odysseus Acanthoplex* (*Odysseus Scourged with Thorns*);

Odysseus Mainomenos (*Odysseus Gone Mad*); Aikhmalôtides (*The Captive Women*); *Aithiopes* (*The Ethiopians*), or *Memnon*; *Akhilleôs Erastai* (*Lovers of Achilles*); *Helenes Apaitesis (Helen's Demand)*; and *Helenes Gamos (Helen's Marriage)*.

His death at ninety-one spawned some strange stories: one says that he died when reciting a long sentence from his *Antigone* without taking a breath; another that he choked while eating grapes at the Anthesteria festival; a third that he died of sheer happiness after winning his final victory at the City Dionysia.

64. The Greeks Have Four Main Words for Love

The Greeks were particular about what sort of love they were giving and getting. There are four separate words for love in ancient Greek: *agápe*, *éros*, *philía*, and *storgē*. Here are the subtle differences and the nuances they represent:

Agápe (ἀγάπη *agápē*) denotes brotherly love, charity; the love of God for man and of man for God. *Agape* can describe love for one's children and for a husband or wife, or partner.

Éros (ἔρως *érōs*) means sexual love and passion and survives in modern Greek as '*erotas*' – meaning 'intimate love'. To Plato, *eros* is love felt for a person, but with contemplation it develops into an appreciation of a person's inner beauty, or even an appreciation of beauty itself. Plato does not see physical attraction as a necessary part of love, hence the modern use of the phrase 'platonic love' to mean 'love without physical attraction'.

Philia (φιλία *philía*) means affectionate regard, friendship; a dispassionate, virtuous love, as conceived by Aristotle. In his *Nicomachean Ethics*, *philia* is loyalty to friends, family, and community, requiring virtue, equality, and familiarity. At the same time *philos* denotes love between family or friends, enjoyment of an activity, enjoyment between lovers. It can describe comradely friendship developed between brothers in arms who fought side by side on the battlefield.

Storgē (στοργή *storgē*) is love and affection particularly of parents and children. It is rarely used in ancient Greek and then almost always as love within a family.

65. Pericles Was 'the First Citizen of Athens'

Thucydides called him 'the first citizen of Athens' and indeed, he did much to confirm Athens as the cultural centre of the ancient Greek world with his energetic promotion of the written word and the visual arts, sculpture and architecture (including the Parthenon). Politically, Pericles turned the Delian League into an Athenian empire, and led Athens' fighting during the first two years of the Peloponnesian War. This golden period from 461 to 429 BC is known as the 'Age of Pericles'.

In 463 BC Cimon, who believed that democracy had run its course, was accused of neglecting Athens' interests in Macedon; Pericles was the chief prosecutor and although Cimon was acquitted this time, Pericles was instrumental in his ostracism two years later for betraying Athens by supporting Sparta. The leader of the pro-democratic party and Pericles' mentor, Ephialtes, had proposed a watering down of the powers of the Areopagus, which the Ecclesia adopted, ushering in a new age of 'radical democracy'.

Ephialtes was assassinated in 461 allowing Pericles to take over as ruler of Athens. Pericles launched his populist social policy: he introduced a decree allowing the poor to attend the theatre free of charge, with the state footing the bill; he lowered the property requirement for the archonship in 457 BC (thus permitting poorer people); and paid wages to all jurymen in the Heliaia from around after 454 BC. His law of 451 BC restricted Athenian citizenship to those people who could prove Athenian parentage on both sides.

Pericles showed his military metal when he led Athens in the First Peloponnesian War in 454 BC. In line with Athenian tradition he married a close relative, with whom he had two sons, Paralus and Xanthippus. In 445 BC,

Pericles divorced this wife for the woman whom he really loved, Aspasia of Miletus. She became his mistress and caused outrage when the couple cohabited as if married. Possibly a former prostitute, Aspasia was something of a celebrity and a rare example of an educated and successful woman exerting herself in Athenian society. Her salons were famous and she hosted a coterie comprising the most prominent writers and thinkers, including Socrates. Predictably, though, she was accused of corrupting Athenian society.

The plague claimed the lives of Pericles's sister and of both sons, Xanthippus and Paralus, the same plague that killed Pericles. Ironically, just before his death the Athenians passed a change in the law of 451 BC allowing his half-Athenian son with Aspasia, Pericles the Younger, to become an Athenian citizen and heir. Whose law is it anyway?

Pericles' enduring legacy is the stunning architecture, which stands today on the Athenian acropolis, the peerless literature and philosophy of his age, and the Funeral Oration recorded by Thucydides, which stands as an emblem for the struggle for democracy, civic pride and patriotism.

66. The Ancient Greeks Believed in Bogeywomen

Witch-lite, the scary bogeywoman, was just as malevolent and equally repulsive as her witchy sisters. Some of Greece's pre-eminent philosophers believed that 'of all wild things, the child is most unmanageable ... the most unruly animal there is. That's why he has to be curbed by a great many bridles'. One of these bridles, apparently endorsed by flustered wet nurses, was the introduction of the bogeywoman into the impressionable imaginations of children in their charge. Bogeywomen often appeared as big bad wolves – precursors of the one that terrified little Red Riding Hood. They ate naughty boys and girls alive and were never without a child freshly devoured in their stomach. In ancient Greece the queen of bogeywomen was Mormo – a horrifying donkey with the legs of a woman – variously a queen of the Lystraegones who had lost her own children and now vengefully murdered others', or a child-eating Corinthian. Another was Empusa, who appeared either as a cow, a donkey or beautiful woman; Empusa could be a beautiful, cannibalistic child-eater. Yet another was Gello, evil female spirit and child snatcher.

The Roman's equivalent to Mormo was Lamia – a sexy Libyan woman whose children by Zeus were murdered by Hera. Like Mormo, she too was a cannibal and exacted revenge by murdering other women's babies, eating them alive. Lamia and Empusa were sometimes described as *phasma* – ghosts, or nightmares.

The bogeywoman and bogeyman reappeared, of course, in the cautionary tales of Victorian and Edwardian Europe.

67. The Funeral Oration of Pericles is One of the World's Greatest Speeches

Our constitution does not copy the laws of neighbouring states; we are rather a pattern to others than imitators ourselves. Its administration favours the many instead of the few; this is why it is called a democracy. If we look to the laws, they afford equal justice to all in their private differences; if no social standing, advancement in public life falls to reputation for capacity, class considerations not being allowed to interfere with merit; nor again does poverty bar the way, if a man is able to serve the state, he is not hindered by the obscurity of his condition. The freedom which we enjoy in our government extends also to our ordinary life...But all this ease in our private relations does not make us lawless as citizens. Against this fear is our chief safeguard, teaching us to obey the magistrates and the laws, particularly such as regard the protection of the injured, whether they are actually on the statute book, or belong to that code which, although unwritten, yet cannot be broken without acknowledged disgrace.

Further, we provide plenty of means for the mind to refresh itself from business. We celebrate games and sacrifices all the year round, and the elegance of our private establishments forms a daily source of pleasure and helps to banish the spleen; while the magnitude of our city draws the produce of the world into our harbour, so that to the Athenian the fruits of other countries are as familiar a luxury as those of his own...

In short, I say that as a city we are the school of Hellas, while I doubt if the world can produce a man who, where he has only himself to depend upon, is equal to so many emergencies, and graced by so happy a versatility, as the Athenian...For Athens alone of her contemporaries is found when tested to be greater than her reputation, and alone gives no occasion to her assailants to blush at the antagonist by whom they have been worsted, or to her subjects to question her title by merit to rule. Rather, the admiration of the present and succeeding ages will be ours, since we have not left our power without witness, but have shown it by mighty proofs; and far from needing a Homer for our panegyrist, or other of his craft whose verses might charm for the moment only for the impression which they gave to melt at the touch of fact, we have forced every sea and land to be the highway of our daring, and everywhere, whether for evil or for good, have left imperishable monuments behind us. Such is the Athens for which these men, in the assertion of their resolve not to lose her, nobly fought and died; and well may every one of their survivors be ready to suffer in her cause.

Thucydides *Peloponnesian War, Book 2.34ff* trans.
© Paul Halsall

68. The Delian League: To 'Avenge the Wrongs They Suffered by Ravaging the Territory of the King [of Persia]'

The Delian League was founded in 478 BC as an alliance of between 150 to 173 Greek city-states under the leadership of Athens, whose objective was to continue the war against the Persians after the Battle of Plataea. In the words of Thucydides, the official aim was to 'avenge the wrongs they suffered by ravaging the territory of the king [of Persia]'. In other words: to get ready for future invasion, to seek revenge against Persia, and to establish how best to divide the spoils of war.

Pericles moved its headquarters from Delos to Athens in 454 BC. Athens, though, monopolised the league's navy for its own purposes, leading to much irritation among the other members and ultimately, in 431 BC, led to the outbreak of the Peloponnesian War. The league was dissolved at the end of the war in 404 BC under Lysander, the victorious Spartan commander.

The League was divided into five fiscal districts:

Thrace (the northern Aegean): sixty-two towns, of which Ainos, Argilos, Mende, Potideia, Samothrace, Scione, Sermylia, Strepsa, Thasos, and Torone paid more than five talents.

Hellespont: forty-five towns, Abydus, Byzantium, Chalkedon, the Chersonese, Cyzicus, Lampsacus, Perinthus, and Selymbria paying more than five talents.

Ionia (the eastern Aegean): thirty-five towns, including Cyme, Ephesus, Erythrae, Miletus, and Teos.

Caria: eighty-one towns, including Camirus, Cnidus, Cos, Ialysus, Lindus, Phaselis, and Telmessus.

The islands: twenty-nine towns, including Andros, Carystus, Chalcis, Eretria, Naxos, and Paros.

There were soon defections: Naxos in 471 and Thasos in 465. Thasos was bullied back into the league after a three-year siege; the walls of Thasos were flattened, Athens confiscated their land and navy; the mines of Thasos were appropriated by Athens, and they had to pay yearly tribute and fines. With the democratic reforms of Ephialtes and Pericles came a major change in Athenian foreign policy: the Spartans were snubbed while Athens allied with her enemies, Argos and Thessaly. Megara deserted the Spartan-led Peloponnesian League and allied with Athens, thus facilitating the construction of a double line of walls across the Isthmus of Corinth and protecting Athens from attack. The Athenians also built the Long Walls connecting the city to the Piraeus making it invulnerable to land attack. Athens started accepting money as dues instead of ships, men and weapons, which allowed Pericles to rebuild the Parthenon. The Delian League was looking increasingly more like an empire than an alliance.

Allies of the league included Inaros (fl. *c.* 460 BC), an Egyptian rebel ruler and the son of a Libyan prince named Psamtik. In 460 BC, he revolted against the Persians and defeated the Persian army commanded by a satrap, Achaemenes. The Persians retreated to Memphis, but the Athenians were finally defeated in 454 BC by the Persian army led by Megabyzus after a two-year siege. Inaros was captured and taken to Susa, where he was crucified in 454 BC.

69. Euripides: 'the Most Tragic of Poets'

Like Sophocles before him, Euripides was prolific to say the least. Something between ninety-two and ninety-five tragedies are attributed to him and others survive as fragments; eighteen have come down to us more or less complete. Aristotle called him 'the most tragic of poets', not just for his doom-laden endings but also for uniquely delving into and exploring the inner lives of his characters and representing mythical heroes as everyday people in extraordinary circumstances. Moses Hadas describes it thus: 'For achieving his end Euripides' regular strategy is a very simple one: retaining the old stories and the great names, as his theatre required, he imagines his people as contemporaries subjected to contemporary kinds of pressures, and examines their motivations, conduct and fate in the light of contemporary problems, usages and ideals.'

Another modern scholar describes Euripides' brand of tragedy as 'in his representation of human suffering Euripides pushes to the limits of what an audience can stand; some of his scenes are almost unbearable'.

Euripides was something of a rebel, sympathising with victims of society and, indeed, women; a number of his plays explore female psychology, including Medea, Phaedra, Hecuba, Creusa, Ion and Orestes in *Orestes*. These words, spoken by his Medea, flew in the face of convention: 'Sooner would I stand three times to face their battles, shield in hand, Than bear one child!' So it is hardly surprising that he was tarred with the same brush as Socrates, widely seen as a corrupting influence.

70. Was Aspasia of Miletus a Prostitute?

If any woman bucked the conventional role played by women in Athenian society and embarrassed the social norms, it was Aspasia of Miletus. She was mistress and partner of Pericles and mother of their son, Pericles the Younger. As we have seen, she ran a salon that became *the* place to go for Athenian intellectuals and was frequented by Socrates among others – contemporaries Plato, Aristophanes and Xenophon all mention her. As was normal in the ancient world with obtrusive and intelligent women, she attracted her fair share of sexual slurs and vilification and gained a reputation as a brothel keeper and a prostitute. It is conceivable, though, that she was a *hetaera*, one of those highly educated, high-class and talented prostitutes who were independent of pimps and dutifully paid their taxes as good 'citizens'.

Aspasia was not immune from the criticisms fired at Pericles and at those close to him at the beginning of the Peloponnesian War. Aspasia was accused of 'corrupting the women of Athens in order to satisfy Pericles' perversions' and was tried for impiety. This upset Pericles quite badly, although she was acquitted – Athenaeus says that Pericles pleaded her case weeping 'more tears than when his life and property were endangered'. The playwright Duris made her responsible for the Athenian attack on Samos in 440 BC, and in 425, Aristophanes parodied the prologue of Herodotus's *Histories,* suggesting that the Archidamian War was caused by Megarians who had abducted two girls from Aspasia's brothel: 'Thus far the evil was not serious and we were the only sufferers. But now some young drunkards go to Megara and carry off the courtesan Simaetha; the Megarians, hurt to the quick, run off in turn with two harlots of the house of Aspasia; and so for three whores Greece is set ablaze.

Then Pericles, aflame with ire on his Olympian height, let loose the lightning, caused the thunder to roll, upset Greece and passed an edict, which ran like the song, That the Megarians be banished both from our land and from our markets and from the sea and from the continent.' (Aristophanes, *The Acharnians*)

It was not all bad press, however; this from the satirist Lucian writing in the second century AD: 'We could choose no better model of wisdom than Milesian Aspasia, the admired of the admirable "Olympian"; her political knowledge and insight, her shrewdness and penetration, shall all be transferred to our canvas in their perfect measure.' (Lucian, *A Portrait Study*, XVII.)

Another famous *hetaera* was Thargelia. Plutarch tells us that she was born in Ionia and 'made her onslaughts upon the most influential men'. Like Aspasia Thargelia was well known for her beauty, grace and wit. Plutarch adds that Thargelia 'attached all her consorts to the King of Persia' spreading Persian sympathy in the cities of Greece through her clients, 'who were men of the greatest power and influence'.

71. Phidias – the Greatest of All Greek Sculptors

Phidias is probably the greatest of all Greek sculptors and was the leading light in the beautification of Athens in the fifth century BC. His statue of Zeus in Olympia is one of the Seven Wonders of the World. Completed around 430, it is Zeus seated on a throne, holding a Nike (goddess of victory) in his right hand and a sceptre in his left. His skin was of ivory, his drapery gold; the surrounding statues and paintings by Panaenos were richly decorated. Olympian Zeus was around seven times bigger than life-size at 42 feet and took up the full height of the temple. It is famously said of Phidias that he alone of all men had seen the exact image of the gods and that, through his work, revealed it to his fellow men. He established for eternity the accepted images of Zeus and Athena.

Phidias became superintendent of public works in the city, also creating the symbol of Athens, the colossal statue of Athena Parthenos; it was completed and dedicated in 438, made of gold and ivory standing 38 feet high. The magnificent goddess stands tall, wearing a tunic, aegis, and helmet and holding a Nike in her outstretched right hand and a spear in her left. A decorated shield and snake were by her side. He was also responsible for the Athena Promachos, a colossal bronze statue of Athena, which stood between the Parthenon and the Propylaea.

He supervised the construction of the Propylaea and the Parthenon. Phidias was, however, embroiled in the same wave of criticism and enmity that dogged Pericles and Aspasia. It was not long before that he was accused of appropriating ivory from the statue of Athena. The charge was unproved, but he was then charged with impiety for depicting images of Pericles and himself on the shield of Athena on the Athena Parthenos. He was jailed and later exiled to Elis, where he worked on the Olympian Zeus, after which the Eleans killed him.

In 1958 archaeologists discovered the workshop at Olympia where Phidias made the gold and ivory Zeus. Shards of ivory as well as terracotta moulds and other equipment for a colossal female statue were excavated along with a black-glaze drinking cup with the inscription 'I belong to Phidias'.

The statue of Athena stood in the Parthenon until the fifth century AD, when it was removed by the Romans to Constantinople. In 1197, Constantinople was devastated by fire, but the destruction wrought by the fire was nothing compared to that visited on the city by the Crusaders. In January 1204, the protovestiarius Alexius Murzuphlus provoked a riot, it is presumed, to intimidate Alexius IV, but only succeeded in destroying Phidias' Athena, which stood in the forum.

An asteroid is named after Phidias.

72. Hippocrates Was the Father of Western Medicine

The Father of Western medicine and founder of the Hippocratic School of Medicine. This medical school revolutionized the practice and teaching of clinical medicine in ancient Greece and established it as a discipline in its own right, distinct from the other fields with which it had been associated, namely theurgy and philosophy. Hippocrates established medicine as a profession. Theurgy is the often magical ritual invocation of a god.

Indeed, Hippocrates was the first person to believe that diseases were caused naturally, not by superstition or the gods. He distinguished medicine from religion, arguing that disease was nothing to do with divine punishment but rather the consequence of environmental factors, diet, and lifestyle.

The Hippocratic School focused on patient care and prognosis, rather than diagnosis. This therapeutic approach was based on 'the healing power of nature' whereby the body has the power to rebalance the four humours and heal itself (*physis*). Disease comes from their disharmony and imbalance. The job of the doctor is to restore health by correcting the imbalance and restoring harmony to the humours. Hippocrates says, 'The body of man has in itself blood, phlegm, yellow bile, and black bile; these make up the nature of the body, and through these he feels pain or enjoys health. Now, he enjoys the most perfect health when these elements are duly proportioned to one another in respect to compounding, power and bulk, and when they are perfectly mingled. Pain is felt when one of these elements is in defect or excess, or is isolated in the body without being compounded with all the others.'

Hippocrates believed that rest and immobilization were crucial. Treatment emphasized keeping the patient sterile: only clean water or wine were used on wounds. Generalized treatments included fasting and drinking apple cider vinegar, believing that 'to eat when you are sick, is to feed your sickness'.

One of the strong points of Hippocratic medicine was its emphasis on prognosis. Drug therapy was in its infancy, and often the most effective thing a doctor could do was assess an illness and predict its likely progression based upon case histories. In the *Phaedrus* Plato tells that Hippocrates taught that a doctor could not understand the nature of the body without an understanding of the whole – holistic medicine, in today's parlance.

Much of what the Hippocratic School espoused is still familiar today in terms of medical training, rigour and professionalism. *On the Physician* recommends that doctors always be well turned out, honest, calm, understanding, and serious. In the operating theatre they should ensure the best in 'lighting, personnel, instruments, positioning of the patient, and techniques of bandaging and splinting'. Fingernails should be trimmed to an exact length. Observation and objective note-taking were of paramount importance for the benefit of colleagues and future doctors. Hippocrates led the way by recording symptoms including complexion, pulse, fever, pains, movement, and excretions. He made use of the all-important family history and of environmental factors.

73. Aristophanes Gives a Unique Picture of the Athens of His Day and of the Athenians

The Father of Comedy, eleven of his thirty plays survive virtually complete and provide a unique picture of the Athens of his day and of the Athenians. When Aristophanes staged his first play, *The Banqueters,* Athens was an aggressive imperial power in the fourth year of the Peloponnesian War. His plays extol the achievements of the older generation (for example the victors at Marathon) and are opposed to the current war with Sparta. The plays are highly critical of war profiteers, such as Cleon. This from the *Acharnians*: 'people among us, and I don't mean the polis, remember this — I don't mean the polis -but wicked little men of a counterfeit kind...' By the time he produced his last play around 386 BC, Athens had been vanquished; its empire evaporated along with its position at the political centre of Greece.

It was customary for all actors in classical Athens to wear masks, but whereas in tragedy these were of stereotypical characters, in Aristophanes and other Old Comedy the masks were often caricatures of actual people. In *The Knights* we hear that the mask makers were too frightened to caricature Cleon, but the audience is clever enough to spot him anyway.

These are the surviving plays of Aristophanes: *The Acharnians,* 425 BC; *The Knights,* 424 BC; *The Clouds,* 423 BC; *The Wasps,* 422 BC; *Peace,* 421 BC; *The Birds,* 414 BC; *Lysistrata,* 411 BC; *Thesmophoriazusae* or *The Women Celebrating the Thesmophoria, c.* 411 BC; *The Frogs,* 405 BC; *Ecclesiazusae* or *The Assemblywomen, c.* 392 BC; *Wealth,* 388 BC.

Aristophanes is the only extant representative of the Old Comedy – that is, of the comic drama in which chorus, mime, and burlesque still played a considerable part and was characterized by fantasy, invective and satire, licentious humour, and political criticism. But Aristophanes belongs to the end of this phase. His last surviving play, which has no choric element at all, is regarded as the only extant specimen of the short-lived Middle Comedy, which, before the end of the fourh century BC, was superseded by the more realistic social satire of the New Comedy.

A good example of Aristophanic Old Comedy is *Lysistrata* written soon after the catastrophic defeat of the Athenian expedition to Sicily in 413. *Lysistrata* depicts the seizure of the Acropolis and of the treasury of Athens by the city's women who, at Lysistrata's instigation, have, together with all the women of Greece, declared a sex strike until such time as the men will make peace.

Famous Aristophanic quotations:

Under every stone lurks a politician.

Men of sense often learn from their enemies. It is from their foes, not their friends, that cities learn the lesson of building high walls and ships of war...

These impossible women! How they do get around us! The poet was right: Can't live with them, or without them.

Youth ages, immaturity is outgrown, ignorance can be educated, and drunkenness sobered, but stupid lasts forever.

Open your mind before your mouth.

74. Voodoo Dolls: the Greeks Stuck Needles in Their Brains

Voodoo dolls were a popular way of binding unpopular people; thirty-eight have been found. They are made from a variety of materials including lead, bronze, and clay as well as wax, wool, and dough. The typical doll demonstrated a number of characteristics, which included: their legs or arms twisted behind the back as if bound; they were impaled with nails; the extremities and/or upper torso may be contorted back to front; they may be confined in a box or similar (coffin?); the doll is inscribed with the name of the victim; it is found in a grave or sanctuary.

As we have seen, some men and women were prepared to go to inordinate lengths to bind and restrain, to guarantee the fidelity of their women and men. This voodoo doll curse (*PGM 4, 296–466*) is one of the most notorious and malevolent. Although it is from fourth century AD Greece, it's surely typical of a practice that had been going on for centuries. It takes a typically prescriptive recipe form: 'take wax or clay from a potter's wheel and form it into two figures, a male and a female ... her arms should be tied behind her back, and she should kneel'. This is supported by some sinister instructions: to 'inscribe magical words on her head and other parts of her body, including the genitals; to stick a needle into her brain, and twelve others into other organs; tie a binding spell written on a lead plate to the figures, dedicate it to gods of the underworld and leave it at sunset near to the tomb of someone who has died violently or prematurely; invite them to rise from the dead and bring X [the object of the charm], daughter of Y, to him and make her love him'. There then follows a litany of evil instructions to deprive the girl of food and drink, sexual intercourse, sleep and health – all designed to make her have sex with the curser in perpetuity. Dehumanisation, ritual abuse – physical, psychological and sexual, subjugation – were the order of the day.

Sarapammon (*Suppl Mag* 47) invokes a whole pantheon of infernal gods in his insane efforts to ensure the fidelity of Ptolemais. He asks the daemon Antinous to bind Ptolemais to stop her from having intercourse or from being sodomised: 'and give no pleasure to any man but me ... and let her not eat, nor drink, nor be happy, nor go out, nor sleep with anyone but me ... drag her by the hair and entrails until she does not reject me ... submissive for her entire life, loving me, desiring me'.

That tablet was found in a vase, fittingly enough in Antinoupolis, which also contained a voodoo-type clay figure of a submissive, kneeling woman, her hands tied behind her back and body pierced with needles – the 'Louvre Doll'. Love is strange.

THE ANCIENT GREEKS IN 100 FACTS

75. Prostitution Was Just as Important as the Institutions of Marriage and Slavery

Prostitution of various kinds was just as important as the institutions of marriage and slavery, and was big business in Athens and in other towns, cities and ports.

On the other hand, adultery with a free woman was frowned upon and dealt with severely: the cuckold had the legal right to kill an adulterer *in flagrante delicto* or a rapist. Female adulterers were deemed prostitutes and forbidden to marry or take part in public ceremonies. However, if the average age of marriage for men was thirty, then, if a young Greek wanted sex, he had little option but to turn to slaves or prostitutes. This was considered acceptable practice.

Philemon describes how Solon regulated sex in Athens:'[Solon], seeing Athens full of young men, with both an instinctive compulsion, and a tendency to stray in an inappropriate direction, bought women and established them in various places, equipped and common to all. The women stand naked so that you get what you see. Have a good look... The door is open. One obol. Pop in. There is no shyness, no idle chat, nor does she recoil. Get stuck in, as you wish, in whatever way you wish. You come out. Tell her to go to hell. You've never met her before.'

What then was on offer?

The *pornai* (πόρναι) were at the bottom end of the ladder owned by pimps or a *pornoboskós* (πορνοβοσκός) working in brothels in 'red-light' districts such as Piraeus or Kerameikos in Athens. Street walkers were next. Sandals with inscribed soles have been excavated, and these left an imprint – 'ΑΚΟΛΟΥΘΕΙ AKOLOUTHEI' (Follow me!) – on the ground. Eubulus, a comic author, describes them: 'plastered over with layers of white lead ... jowls smeared with mulberry juice. And if you go out on a summer's day, two rills of inky water flow from your eyes, and the sweat rolling from your cheeks upon your throat makes a vermilion furrow, while the hairs blown about on your faces look grey, they are so full of white lead'.

Young virgins could charge more, as could the pretty prostitute – unlike her older, jaded colleague. Exclusivity (difficult to police) cost more, as did group sex. Musicians and dancing girls working the banquets were the next category. At the top end were the *hetaerae* who, as we have seen, were often intelligent and attractive high-class whores.

Many *hetaerae* were exceedingly well connected: Aspasia apart, we can name Theodota, companion of Alcibiades; Naeara, the subject of a discourse of Pseudo-Demosthene; Phryne, the model for Praxiteles' Aphrodite of Knidos, she was his mistress but also friend to the orator Hypereides, who defended her against a charge of impiety; and Leontium, companion of Epicurus and herself a philosopher. Pythionice was the mistress of Harpalus, Alexander the Great's treasurer; and Thaïs was Alexander's mistress and then Ptolemy I's after him.

76. Avoiding Pregnancy for a Prostitute Was Paramount

What do we know about the sex life of a Greek prostitute? Greek, like Latin, is rich in words for a prostitute. One is *khamaitypés* (χαμαιτυπής), which literally means 'one who hits the ground', suggesting their sex took place on the ground. Much of the vilification they attracted derives from their venality, a popular theme in Greek comedy, and the fact that prostitutes were the only Athenian women who handled money. Furthermore, a grasping approach to life is hardly surprising: a prostitute's career was short-lived. Youth and physical attraction were everything, so income diminished over time. To compensate and to provide for old age, prostitutes had to acquire as much money as possible in a very limited window of opportunity.

Avoiding pregnancy was obviously paramount. Hippocrates has one of the few descriptions of contraception, in his *On the Seed*. Here he details the case of a dancer 'who had the habit of going with the men'. He recommends that she 'jump up and down, touching her buttocks with her heels at each leap' to evacuate the sperm. *Pornai* may have had recourse to abortion or infanticide.

Greek pottery also tells us something of the daily life of prostitutes through banquet scenes, sexual activities, toilet scenes and scenes showing abuse. In the toilet scenes the prostitute tends to have sagging breasts, flabby rolls of flesh and the like – one kylix shows a prostitute urinating into a pot. For sexual acts, the presence of a prostitute is often denoted by a purse, and the sexual position most frequently shown is the leapfrog – or sodomy where the woman is 'folded in two' with her hands flat on the ground. A number of vases show abuse, where the prostitute is threatened with a stick or sandal, and forced to perform acts considered degrading by the Greeks: fellatio, sodomy or sex with two partners.

There were also many male prostitutes, some of whom had a female clientele. Most, however, serviced male customers.

Temple prostitution seems to have been rife. Strabo describes female temple servants in the temple of Aphrodite in Corinth: 'The temple of Aphrodite was so rich that it employed more than a thousand hetairas, [14] whom both men and women had given to the goddess.' Many people visited the town on account of them, and thus these hetairas contributed to the riches of the town: for the ship captains frivolously spent their money there, hence the saying: 'The voyage to Corinth is not for every man.'

In 464 BC, Xenophon, a citizen of Corinth who was a famous runner and winner of the pentathlon at the Olympic Games, dedicated 100 young girls to the temple of the goddess as a sign of thanksgiving. This act of generosity is described in a hymn that Pindar was commissioned to write celebrating 'the very welcoming girls, servants of Peïtho and luxurious Corinth'.

77. THE PELOPONNESIAN WAR MARKED THE END OF ATHENS AS A POLITICAL AND MILITARY FORCE

At the close of the seventh century BC, Sparta was the most powerful *polis* in the Peloponnese, followed by Argos. The *poleis* of Corinth and Elis allied with Sparta while other Peloponnesian states followed until only Argos and Achaea remained outside what became the Peloponnesian League.

Sparta was the hegemon, and controlled the council of allies, which comprised the assembly of Spartiates and the Congress of Allies. Each state had one vote regardless of size or power. Tribute was paid only during wars, when one third of the military capacity of a member could be requested. Alliances with outsiders could be made with Sparta alone.

After the Persian Wars the league developed into the Hellenic League to include Athens and other states. Sparta pulled out to reform the Peloponnesian League with its original allies. The Hellenic League then became the Athenian-led Delian League. The two leagues clashed in the Peloponnesian War.

We can divide the Peloponnesian War into three phases. The first phase, the Archidamian War, saw Sparta repeatedly invade Attica around Athens, while Pericles' strategy was for Athens's navy to repeatedly raid the coast of the Peloponnese. The Spartan king Archidamus II thus deprived Athens of the productive land around their city, but the city still had access to the sea. Many citizens abandoned their farms and (fatally) moved inside the Long Walls, which connected Athens to its port of Piraeus. At the end of the first year of the war, Pericles delivered his famous Funeral Oration (431 BC). The following year plague struck Athens, spreading relentlessly and remorselessly through the packed city. The plague was a major cause of Athens's defeat: it exterminated over 30,000 citizens, sailors and soldiers, including Pericles and his sons. Between one-third and two-thirds of the Athenian population died. Athenian manpower was drastically diminished and even foreign mercenaries refused to hire themselves out to a city on its knees with plague. Sparta abandoned its invasion of Attica fearing infection.

The Archidamian War ended in 421 with the Peace of Nicias. The peace, however, did not last, with renewed hostilities in the Peloponnese. In 415 BC, Athens sent a huge expeditionary force to attack Syracuse; the attack was a calamity for Athens and the entire force was destroyed in 413 BC. The Decelean, or the Ionian, War followed with Sparta bolstered by support from Persia, rebellions among Athens' allies in the Aegean and Ionia, and the loss of Athenian naval supremacy. The war effectively came to an end with the destruction of Athens's fleet at Aegospotami, after which Athens surrendered.

This marked the end of Athens as a political and military force. Sparta, on the other hand, took over as the leading power. Poverty was everywhere in the Peloponnese, while the city of Athens was devastated. Civil war among *poleis* was endemic.

Thucydides saw it all coming: 'The growth of the power of Athens, and the alarm which this inspired in Lacedaemon [Sparta], made war inevitable.'

78. THUCYDIDES WAS THE FATHER OF 'SCIENTIFIC HISTORY'

Major Athenian historian, political philosopher and general (*strategos*) famous for his *History of the Peloponnesian War,* a defining work of history that has led to Thucydides being called the father of 'scientific history' because of his rigorous research, reliance on eye-witness accounts, evidence gathering and analysis of cause and effect. Unlike the work of Herodotus, Thucydides' history is devoid of interventions by the gods. He omits the arts, literature or the social circumstances in which the events take place focusing instead on actual events, excluding what he may have seen as frivolous or irrelevant.

His Melian Dialogue is a seminal work of international relations theory espousing political realism while Pericles' Funeral Oration is still widely studied in political theory, history, and classical studies and formed the basis for Abraham Lincoln's *Gettysburg Address* during the American Civil War in 1863. The Funeral Oration is one of many speeches in which the historian does not report verbatim but gives us the gist of what was said, or should have been said.

Thucydides interpolates the Melian Dialogue at the invasion of Melos by Athens in 416 BC, dramatizing the negotiations between the Athenians and the rulers of Melos. The Athenians demanded that Melos submit and pay tribute or be destroyed, appealing to the Melians' pragmatism, citing the overwhelming odds they faced. The Melians, on the other hand, appealed to the Athenians' sense of decency and fear of the gods. Result: stalemate, so the Athenians subdued Melos and slaughtered or enslaved the Melians.

79. Plague in Athens: Ebola Hemorrhagic Fever?

Thucydides' description of the plague in Athens is a shockingly realistic and vivid account of a disaster, the like of which the city had never suffered before. Its appearance so soon after the stirring and patriotic Funeral Oration lends it even more realism and horror in its description of the frailty of human life.

Symptoms included: 'people in good health were all of a sudden attacked by violent heats in the head, and redness and inflammation in the eyes, the inward parts, such as the throat or tongue, becoming bloody and emitting an unnatural and fetid breath ... followed by sneezing and hoarseness, after which the pain soon reached the chest, and produced a hard cough. When it fixed in the stomach, it upset it; and discharges of bile of every kind named by physicians ensued... In most cases also an ineffectual retching followed. Though many lay unburied, birds and beasts would not touch them, or died after tasting them [...]. The bodies of dying men lay one upon another, and half-dead creatures reeled about the streets and gathered round all the fountains in their longing for water. The sacred places also in which they had quartered themselves were full of corpses of persons who had died there, just as they were; for, as the disaster passed all bounds, men, not knowing what was to become of them, became equally contemptuous of the gods' property and the gods' dues. All the burial rites before in use were entirely upset, and they buried the bodies as best they could. Many from want of the proper appliances, through so many of their friends having died already, had recourse to the most shameless sepultures: sometimes getting the start of those who had raised a pile, they threw their own dead body upon the stranger's pyre and ignited it; sometimes they tossed the corpse which they were carrying on the top of another that was burning, and so went off.'

We have already noted the devastating and debilitating effect of the plague on Athens' military capability during the Peloponnesian War. There have been various suggestions as to what the plague actually was, including ebola hemorrhagic fever, glanders, typhus, typhoid, anthrax, measles, and toxic shock syndrome or smallpox. These are, however, pointless as Thucydides himself declares: 'All speculation as to its origin and its causes, if causes can be found adequate to produce so great a disturbance, I leave to other writers, whether lay or professional; for myself, I shall simply set down its nature, and explain the symptoms by which perhaps it may be recognized by the student, if it should ever break out again. This I can the better do, as I had the disease myself, and watched its operation in the case of others.'

80. PLATO IS *THE* HEART OF CLASSICAL GREEK PHILOSOPHY

Plato is at the heart, if indeed he is not *the* heart, of classical Greek philosophy, and of Western philosophy in general. He was a student of Socrates and the teacher of Aristotle. He was influenced by Heraclitus, Parmenides, and the Pythagoreans as well as by Socrates. He was the founder of the Academy in Athens, the first institution of higher education and learning in the Western world. He was one of the founding fathers of Western religion and spirituality, which Nietzsche called 'Platonism for the people'. He was a great influence on St Augustine of Hippo, pre-eminent philosopher and theologian in the history of Christianity. Plato pioneered the dialogue and dialectic forms in philosophy and is the father of Western political philosophy: the *Republic* and *Laws* in particular give us some of the earliest treatments of political questions from a philosophical perspective. As a mathematician he also paved the way for Euclid's systematic approach to mathematics. The dialogue device enabled him to be detached from the arguments he presented.

Early dialogues are devoted to investigation of a single issue and include the Ευθυφρων (*Euthyphro*) – the Απολογημα (*Apology*) which describes the philosophical life as Socrates presented it in his own defense before the Athenian jury. The Κριτων (Crito) uses Socrates's incarceration to ask whether an individual citizen is ever justified in refusing to obey the state. The *piéce de résistance* of Plato's middle dialogues is his Πολιτεια (Republic), which opens with a Socratic conversation about the nature of justice and progresses to an extended discussion of the virtues (αρετη) of justice (Δικαιωσυνη), wisdom (σοφια), courage (ανδρεια), and moderation (σωφρσυνη) as they manifest both in individuals and in society as a whole. 'This plan for the ideal society or person requires detailed accounts of human knowledge and of the kind of educational program by which it may be achieved by men and women alike, captured in a powerful image of the possibilities for human life in the allegory of the cave. The dialogue concludes with a review of various forms of government, an explicit description of the ideal state in which only philosophers are fit to rule, and an attempt to show that justice is better than injustice.' Among other middle dialogues are Plato's treatments of human emotion in general and of love, in particular in the Φαιδρος (*Phaedrus*) and Συμποσιον (*Symposium*).

Later dialogues include a critical examination of the theory of forms in Παρμενιδης (*Parmenides*), a discussion of the problem of knowledge in Θεαιτητοσ (*Theaetetus*), cosmological speculations in Τιμαιος (*Timaeus*), and a prolix expatiation on government in the unfinished Λεγεις (*Laws*).

Some wise Platonic quotations:

A wise man speaks because he has something to say; a fool because he has to say something.

One of the penalties for refusing to participate in politics is that you end up being governed by your inferiors.

Our love for our children springs from the soul's greatest yearning for immortality.

The greatest penalty of evil-doing is to grow into the likeness of a bad man.

81. SOCRATES NEVER WROTE A WORD

Socrates never put pen to paper: his work is known to us only through the works of Plato and Xenophon, and the plays of Aristophanes. He was an irritation to the Athenian government – an annoying gadfly – and was eventually imprisoned. At his trial, Socrates was asked to name his own punishment: he suggested a wage paid by the government and free dinners for the rest of his life to compensate for the time he spent as Athens's benefactor. This was to no avail. Socrates was found guilty of corrupting the minds of the youth of Athens and of impiety; he was sentenced to death by drinking a concoction containing hemlock.

The trial of Socrates is the salient, unifying event in many Platonic dialogues. In the *Apology*, Socrates defends himself against those charges of impiety and corruption of the young. Five dialogues foreshadow the trial: the *Theaetetus* and the *Euthyphro*; in the *Meno*, one of the men who brings legal charges against Socrates, Anytus, warns him about the trouble he may get into if he continues to criticize influential people; in the *Gorgias*, Socrates says that his trial will be a farce, like that of a doctor prosecuted by a cook who asks a jury made up of children to choose between the doctor's bitter medicine and the cook's tasty morsels (521e–522a). In the *Republic* (7.517e), Socrates explains why an enlightened man will always fail in a courtroom situation. The *Apology* is Socrates's defence speech, and the *Crito* and *Phaedo* are set in prison after his conviction.

Xanthippe was Socrates's first wife and mother of their three sons, Lamprocles, Sophroniscus, and Menexenus. She was forty years or so younger than Socrates. From Plato's *Phaedo* and Xenophon's *Memorabilia*, we learn that she was a devoted wife and mother. From Xenophon's

Symposium, Socrates tells us why he chose her: 'None of your soft-mouthed, docile animals for me,' he says, 'the horse for me to own must show some spirit', confident that if he can manage such an animal, every other horse will be a pushover. Xanthippe was so enraged with her husband on one occasion that she took a full chamber pot and poured it out over Socrates's head, to which the philosopher's resigned reaction was to say, 'After thunder comes the rain.' Xanthippe has since come to mean a nagging, shrewish wife and in Shakespeare's *Taming of the Shrew*, Petruchio compares Katherina 'As Socrates' Xanthippe or worse' in Act 1 Scene 2.

Some Socratic quotations:

True knowledge exists in knowing that you know nothing.

I know that I am intelligent, because I know that I know nothing.

By all means marry: if you get a good wife, you'll become happy; if you get a bad one, you'll become a philosopher.

I cannot teach anybody anything, I can only make them think.

To find yourself, think for yourself.

82. ARISTOTLE IS THE WORLD'S FIRST GREAT POLYMATH

Aristotle is the world's first great polymath and has made huge contributions to our understanding of logic, metaphysics, mathematics, physics, biology, botany, ethics, politics, agriculture, medicine, dance and theatre.

Aristotle wrote around 200 treatises, of which only thirty-one are extant – unfortunately they are in the form of lecture notes and draft manuscripts never intended for publication, so they do not reflect the reputed polished prose style that impressed many Greeks and Romans, including Cicero. Aristotle founded the Lyceum, another school of learning based in Athens. He tutored Alexander the Great.

These surviving works can be categorised as follows and demonstrate the sheer breadth of his output: Logic; Physics (change, motion, void, time); On the Heavens (structure of heaven, earth, elements); On Generation (through combining material constituents); Meteorologics (origin of comets, weather, disasters).

Psychology: On the Soul (faculties, senses, mind, imagination); On Memory, Reminiscence, Dreams, and Prophesying;

Natural history: History of Animals (physical/mental qualities, habits); On the parts of Animals; On the Movement of Animals; On the Progression of Animals; On the Generation of Animals.

Philosophical works: Metaphysics (substance, cause, form, potentiality); Nicomachean Ethics (soul, happiness, virtue, friendship); Eudemain Ethics; Magna Moralia.

Politics: (best states, utopias, constitutions, revolutions);

Rhetoric: (elements of forensic and political debate); Poetics (tragedy, epic poetry).

Aristotle's views on women can be found in his *Politics*: 'The male, unless constituted in some respect contrary to nature, is by nature more expert at leading than the female, and the elder and complete than the younger and incomplete' (1259a41). To Aristotle it is natural for the male to rule: 'The relation of male to female is by nature a relation of superior to inferior and ruler to ruled' (1245b12). 'The slave is wholly lacking the deliberative element; the female has it but it lacks authority; the child has it but it is incomplete' (1260a11).

Not surprisingly, some have accused Aristotle of misogyny and sexism. However, it must be said that Aristotle did give equal weight to women's happiness as he did to men's.

Education was paramount: 'That the legislator must, therefore, make the education of the young his object above all would be disputed by no one (1337a10)... Since there is a single end for the city as a whole, it is evident that education must necessarily be one and the same for all, and that the superintendence of it should be common and not on a private basis... For common things the training too should be made common' (1337a21).

His work in zoology has been called the grandest biological synthesis of the time, and remained the ultimate authority for many centuries after his death. His observations on the anatomy of octopus, cuttlefish, crustaceans, and many other marine invertebrates are remarkably accurate, and could only have been made from first-hand experience with dissection. Aristotle described the embryological development of a chick; he distinguished whales and dolphins from fish; he described the chambered stomachs of ruminants and the social organization of bees.

83. The Stoics and the Epicureans Founded the Academy and the Garden

Stoicism was a school of philosophy founded in Athens by Zeno of Citium in the early third century BC. Zeno established the Stoic Academy (Stoa) in Athens.

The Stoic doctrine is essentially divided into three parts: logic, physics, and ethics. It is a system of ethics that is guided by logic, and has physics as its base. Their morality is ascetic, involving a life led in accordance with nature and controlled by virtue, teaching utter indifference (*apathea*) to everything external, for nothing external could be either good or evil. So, to the Stoics both pain and pleasure, penury and wealth, sickness and health, were equally unimportant.

The Stoic philosophers were nothing if not socially unconventional. They argued for equality of the sexes – sexual inequality to them was contrary to the laws of nature. In teaching this, they followed the Cynics, who believed that men and women should dress identically and be educated in the same way. Stoics saw marriage as companionship between equals rather than a biological or social necessity, and practiced this as well as preaching it.

Epicureanism was a system of philosophy based upon the teachings of the philosopher Epicurus, founded around 307 BC along with his school, the Garden. The Garden was quite liberal, including women and slaves among its members. Some were also vegetarians like Epicurus, but not eating meat was never a stipulation.

Epicurus was an atomic materialist, a disciple of Democritus and an opponent of superstition and divine intervention. Epicurus believed that pleasure is the greatest good, but that paradoxically, the road to attaining this pleasure is to live modestly, to gain knowledge of the ways of the world and the limit one's desires. This led to a state of calm (*ataraxia*) and freedom from fear, as well as absence of physical pain (*aponia*). The combination of these two states was thought to constitute happiness in its highest form. Epicurus explains it in his *Letter to Menoeceus*: 'When we say ... that pleasure is the end and aim, we do not mean the pleasures of the prodigal or the pleasures of sensuality, as we are understood to do by some through ignorance, prejudice or wilful misrepresentation. By pleasure we mean the absence of pain in the body and of trouble in the soul. It is not by an unbroken succession of drinking bouts and of revelry, not by sexual lust, nor the enjoyment of fish and other delicacies of a luxurious table, which produce a pleasant life; it is sober reasoning, searching out the grounds of every choice and avoidance, and banishing those beliefs through which the greatest tumults take possession of the soul.'

Epicurean quotes:

Of all the things which wisdom has contrived which contribute to a blessed life, none is more important, more fruitful, than friendship – quoted by Cicero.

Don't fear god,

Don't worry about death;

What is good is easy to get, and

What is terrible is easy to endure – quoted by Philodemus.

84. SEX WAS OFTEN NEVER FAR AWAY AT A SYMPOSIUM

An important Greek social institution, the symposium (from the Greek: συμπόσιον from συμπίνειν, 'to drink together') was a drinking party and, in ancient Greece, formed the setting for two Socratic dialogues, Plato's *Symposium* and Xenophon's *Symposium*, as well featuring in the elegies of Theognis of Megara. It was much more than just 'a lad's night out' – rather, it was a way for men of respected families to celebrate the introduction of young men into aristocratic society, and to make most of other special occasions, such as victories in athletic and drama or poetry contests.

Symposia would typically be held in the *andrōn* (ἀνδρών), the men's quarters. The symposiasts would recline on between seven and nine pillowed couches set against three walls of the room making between fourteen and twenty-seven drinkers. In Macedonian symposia the emphasis was not just on drinking but hunting too, and young men were allowed to recline and imbibe only after they had killed their first wild boar.

Catering included food and, obviously, wine. There was entertainment, which could include games, songs, flute girls or boys, and slaves doing various things. Often sex of one kind or another would not be far away. High-class female prostitutes (*hetairai*) and entertainers were hired to perform and converse with the guests. Among the instruments in the women's repertoire was the *aulos*, a kind of oboe, and the stringed barbiton. The most famous symposium is described in Plato's dialogue of the same name and hosted by the poet Agathon to mark his first victory at the drama contest of the 416 BC city Dionysia. Amusingly, Plato tells us that the celebration was upstaged by the surprise entrance of the young buck

Alcibiades, dropping in drunk and half naked, the flotsam of an earlier symposium.

The most important man at any symposium was the symposiarch. It was he who would decide the strength of the wine and its dilution, depending on whether serious discussions were on the agenda or just indulgence. In Greece, wine was only drunk after the dinner, and women were barred.

In a fragment from his *c.* 375 BC play *Semele*, Eubulus has the god of wine Dionysus describe for us the right and wrong way to drink: 'For sensible men I prepare only three kraters: one for health (which they drink first), the second for love and pleasure, and the third for sleep. After the third one is drained, wise men go home. The fourth krater is not mine any more - it belongs to bad behaviour; the fifth is for shouting; the sixth is for rudeness and insults; the seventh is for fights; the eighth is for breaking the furniture; the ninth is for depression; the tenth is for madness and unconsciousness.'

It was the role of the symposiarch to stop things from getting out of hand, but Greek literature and art tell us that the third krater limit was not always observed. *Plus ça change.*

85. Philip II of Macedon Introduced the Phalanx

Philip II can take credit for elevating a small kingdom on the edge of classical Greece to one which dominated the Greek world – all within twenty-five years, between 359 and 336 BC. Legend has it that Macedonia emerged in the eighth or early seventh century BC under the Argead dynasty, who migrated to the region from the Greek city of Argos in Peloponnesus. Eventually, a Macedonian state was set up by King Amyntas III (*c.* 393–370 BC); unlike most of the rest of Greece, though, Macedon retained a hereditary monarchy with absolute power. Amyntas had three sons, including Alexander II and Perdiccas III, who reigned only briefly. Perdicca's infant heir was disposed of by Amyntas' third son, Philip II, who declared himself king.

Philip was king of Macedon from 359 BC until he was assassinated in 336. He had his work cut out on his accession, to prevent his kingdom from being carved up between hostile neighbours. Philip was responsible for a long period of Macedonian aggression and expansion; he received his military education while hostage in Thebes. One of his first acts was to crush the 3,000 Athenian hoplites who had landed at Methoni. He expanded into the territory of the Paeonians, Thracians, and Illyrians and annexed Pelagonia and southern Paeonia.

His great contribution to classical warfare was the introduction of the phalanx infantry and their *sarisa*, a 12-cubit-long long pike. From 358 he won a series of battles against Illyria (at Lake Lychnitis) Athens and Thrace. He took the Thracian settlement of Crenides and the nearby gold mines, which netted him 1,000 talents per year and a very healthy war chest. In 353 in the Third Sacred War he invaded Thessaly, defeating 7,000 Phocians and, despite two defeats, returned to Thessaly in 352 with an army of 20,000 infantry and 3,000 cavalry as well as the entire Thessalian army. In the Battle of Crocus Field he slew 6,000 Phocians; 3,000 more were taken prisoner and later drowned as temple robbers. Justin tells us that Philip sent his men into battle wearing crowns of laurel, the symbol of Apollo, 'as if he was the avenger ... of sacrilege, and he proceeded to battle under the leadership, as it were, of the god'. In 348 he took Olynthus and two years later was in control of Thermopylae.

In 342 BC Philip moved against the Scythians, taking Eumolpia and renaming it Philippopolis (modern Plovdiv). In 340 Philip he besieged Perinthus and in 339 the city of Byzantium, but both failed. However, he defeated the Thracians in the Hebrus Valley, and an alliance of Thebans and Athenians at the Battle of Chaeronea in 338 BC; in the same year he destroyed Amfissa. Philip was now in control of most of Greece.

Philip set up the League of Corinth in 337 BC as *hegemon* and was elected leader of the army assembled to invade the Persian Empire. However, in 336 BC Philip was assassinated, and was succeeded on the throne of Macedon by his son Alexander III, better known to us as Alexander the Great.

86. Alexander the Great Was Undefeated in Battle

Alexander succeeded his father aged twenty and spent the best part of his reign on a never-ending military campaign through Asia and northeast Africa; by the time he was thirty he had forged one of the largest empires of the ancient world, extending from Greece to Egypt into north-west India and what is today Pakistan. He remained undefeated in battle and lives on as one of history's most successful military commanders still studied in military academies around the world. He was tutored by Aristotle from the age of thirteen.

Alexander took over his father's mantle and broke the Persian Empire, which then extended from Asia Minor, and Syria to Egypt, in a series of battles, the most decisive being Issus and Gaugamela.

This pre-battle speech at Issus, recorded by Q. Curtius Rufus, is typical: 'Riding to the front line he (Alexander) named the soldiers and they responded from spot to spot where they were lined up. The Macedonians, who had won so many battles in Europe and set off to invade Asia ... got encouragement from him – he reminded them of their permanent values. They were the world's liberators and one day they would pass the frontiers set by Hercules and Father Liber. They would subdue all races on Earth. Bactria and India would become Macedonian provinces. Getting closer to the Greeks, he reminded them that those were the people (the Persians on the other side) who provoked war with Greece ... those were the people that burned their temples and cities ... As the Illyrians and Thracians lived mainly from plunder, he told them to look at the enemy line glittering in gold...'

Alexander took his army on an expedition covering 11,000 miles, founding over seventy cities and creating an empire that stretched over three continents and covered around 2 million square miles. Greece in the west, north of the Danube, south of Egypt and as far east as the Indian Punjab were all now interconnected in a huge international political and commercial network united by a common Greek language and culture, while the king himself adopted foreign customs in order to rule his millions of ethnically diverse subjects.

In 327 BC Alexander invaded the Punjab. At the battle of the River Hydaspes, against King Porus, Alexander's army crossed the heavily defended river during a thunderstorm to oppose Porus' forces. The Indians were defeated despite their deployment of terrifying elephants, a monster the Macedonians had never set eyes on before.

Alexander died of a fever in Babylon in 323 BC before he could carry out his planned invasion of the Arabian Peninsula. His legacy is formidable: he founded twenty cities, which were subsequently given his name, including cosmopolitan Alexandria in Egypt. We have him largely to thank for the Hellenistic age and the Hellenistic culture which suffused the Mediterranean world. Alexander left no heirs, so in the power vacuum remaining after his death the empire he had fought so hard to build up was gradually dismembered by the feuding generals known as the Diadochi.

87. Tarentum Was Once One of the Largest Cities in the World

Greece, however, along with the rest of the Mediterranean world, was now faced with another external rival. The Romans had been systematically overcoming rivals in Italy to take control of the peninsula. Roman attention now turned to the city-states and colonies of Greece. It was during the subsequent conflicts that the elephant was first deployed in the Mediterranean theatre as a weapon of mass destruction, and in which the term 'pyrrhic' victory was coined.

The Pyrrhic War was triggered by a minor naval battle in the Bay of Tarentum and the treaty obligations between the city of Tarentum and Epirus in Greece. When Rome entered Tarentine waters, Tarentum saw this as a breach of treaty and requested payback from Pyrrhus for the aid they had given the Greek king in his conflict with Korkyra. Pyrrhus saw this as an empire-building opportunity.

Tarentum ('the Spartan City') was founded in 706 BC by Dorian Greek immigrants and was the only colony to be established by the Spartans. In 500 BC the city was one of the largest in the world with up to 300,000 people.

Tarentum's commercial supremacy came about largely through its extensive sheep farming industry – its fleeces, dyed purple with the copious mussels obtainable from the harbour, were much sought after throughout Italy. This commercial prowess was matched by political stability and the ability to raise an army of some 15,000 men, alongside the strongest navy in the Mediterranean. The Tarentine armed forces were strengthened by numerous Greek mercenaries, allowing them to fend off incursions by the Oscans and even attempt expansion. During the First Samnite War the Tarentines formed an alliance with King Archidamus of Sparta and then, in 334 BC, with his brother-in-law, King Alexander of Epirus. Alexander successfully quelled incursions by the Brutii, Samnites and Lucanians and forged a non-aggression pact with the Romans on behalf of Tarentum. Tarentum, however, was increasingly suspicious of Alexander's ambitions and left him to hang out to dry and to be slaughtered by the Lucanians. Rome's expansionism, too, was viewed with some anxiety, with Rome's attempts at diplomacy rejected by Tarentum. The Battle of Tarentum followed soon after.

The naval battle erupted when the Roman admiral, Lucius Valerius, entered the Bay of Tarentum with a small flotilla and dropped anchor; he was assuming the Tarentines to be friendly and that all previous treaty obligations were null and void. Valerius sailed into Tarentine waters in response to a plea from the Greek city of Thurii on the Gulf of Otranto for military assistance against the Lucanians. This action violated a treaty between Rome and Tarentum, forbidding Rome from entering Tarentine waters. The Tarentines had been agitating against the Romans and saw Valerius' presence as a threat; accordingly, they attacked the Roman fleet and sank Valerius' flagship and other vessels. The Romans, to contain the outrage, tried diplomacy, but their claims for compensation were spurned by Tarentum. Rome then declared war on Tarentum.

88. Pyrrhus Gave His Name to a Pointless Victory

Pyrrhus was crowned king of Epirus (r. 306–302, 297–272 BC) and Macedon (r. 288–284, 273–272 BC). He was the son of Aeacides and Phthia, a Thessalian woman who was second cousin of Alexander the Great, through Alexander's mother, Olympias. In 298 BC Pyrrhus was taken hostage to Alexandria, in a peace treaty between Demetrius, his brother-in-law, and Ptolemy I Soter. There, he married Ptolemy I's step-daughter, Antigone, and regained his kingdom in Epirus in 297 BC with aid from Ptolemy I. Pyrrhus had his co-ruler Neoptolemus II of Epirus murdered. One of the more flamboyant of Greek brigands whose services were readily available throughout the Mediterranean, Pyrrhus answered Tarentum's plea for support against Rome with alacrity.

There was consternation and terror when the Romans saw what they were up against at the Heraclea. Valerius Laevinus, with a lesser force of 20,000 men, crossed the River Siris, but his army crumbled in the face of a 3,000-strong cavalry charge followed by infantry. The Romans were finally defeated when Pyrrhus' elephants panicked the Roman horses and the Thessalian cavalry routed the astonished Roman troops. Pyrrhus, despite his victory, lost 13,000 men to the Romans' 15,000, although the figures may be nearer 7,000 and 4,000. The Lucanians and the Samnites joined Pyrrhus on the strength of this victory.

The huge losses suffered here by Pyrrhus give us the term 'Pyrrhic victory' where casualties are so great in victory that the damage is greater than any gain. Pyrrhus, recognising his dilemma, is reputed to have commented, '*Ne ego si iterum eodem modo uicero, sine ullo milite Epirum reuertar*': 'Another victory like that and I'll be going back to Epirus without a single soldier,' and 'If we win one more battle with the Romans, we shall be utterly ruined.'

'Friendly fire' would have been a common occurrence in the head-on, close-combat fighting of the tight-knit Greek and Roman fighting units. The absence of distinctive uniforms, similar languages between enemies and allies, and the general turmoil would have heightened the chances of fighting or raining missiles down on friends and allies. Thucydides had vividly described the mayhem of the Athenian defeat at the night-time Battle of Epipolae in 413 BC – a blueprint for battlefield confusion. He asks how anyone can really know what is going on in the dark: 'many parts of the enemy ended by falling upon each other, friend against friend, citizen against citizen'. This nightmare scenario must have been repeated endlessly down the years. Despite attempts to control and to deter, the elephant only added to the opportunities for 'friendly fire'. Despite its benefits as a psychologic and physical instrument of war, the cumbersome beast was prone to panic, difficult to control and indiscriminately deadly when on the rampage. Time and time again when a startled, frightened elephant turned and fled, it trampled its own soldiers in its blind rush to flee the field of battle.

89. The Elephant Was the First Weapon of Mass Destruction

So, the Pyrrhic Wars were also notable for the first deployments of elephants (elephantries) by the Greeks against the Roman army. The Indians were the first to use the elephant as an instrument of war, where they make an appearance in the Sanskrit epics, later stories of the Mahabharata and the Ramayana the fourth century BC. To some kings an army without elephants was as unacceptable as a forest without a lion, a kingdom without a king or valour unaided by weapons. Their use spread westwards to the Persians in their wars with Alexander the Great. The first confrontation came at the Battle of Gaugamela in 331 BC, when the Persians deployed fifteen elephants. They made such an impact that Alexander sacrificed to the god of fear on the eve of the battle, but according to some sources the elephants ultimately failed to deploy in the final battle owing to fatigue from their long march the day before. Alexander was victorious and so impressed by this novel war machine that he enlisted the captured fifteen into his own army, adding to the complement as he overran the rest of Persia. Up against Porus, in the modern-day Punjabi region of Pakistan, Alexander faced up to 100 war elephants at the Battle of the Hydaspes River, small fry compared to what the kings of the Nanda Empire (Maghada) and Gangaridai (present-day Bangladesh and the Indian state of West Bengal) could throw against him: between 3,000 and 6,000 war elephants, which effectively halted Alexander's invasion of India. Returning home, he set up a unit of elephants to guard his palace at Babylon, and established the office of elephantarch to take command of his elephants. War elephants made their European debut in 318 BC when Polyperchon, one of Alexander's generals, besieged Megalopolis with the help of sixty elephants. Pyrrhus must be given credit for the introduction of the combat elephant to Italy, at the Battle of Heraclea. Here the elephants were of the Indian variety and were given the sobriquet 'Lucanian oxen' by the awestruck Roman soldiers.

The Battle of Raphia (the Battle of Gaza) was fought in 217 BC near modern Rafah between Ptolemy IV Philopator, king and pharaoh of Egypt, and Antiochus III the Great of the Seleucid Empire during the Syrian Wars. It was one of the largest battles fought by the Hellenistic kingdoms and was one of the largest battles of the ancient world. Polybius records that Ptolemy had 70,000 infantry, 5,000 cavalry, and 73 war elephants and Antiochus 62,000 infantry, 6,000 cavalry, and 102 elephants. This is the only battle we know of in which African and Asian elephants were used against each other. Ptolemy's elephants were the now-extinct North African Forest elephants from what is now Eritrea; those of Antiochus were the larger Asian elephants, brought from India. According to Polybius, the African elephants could not bear the smell, sound and sight of their Indian counterparts as well as their greater size and strength, and would flee.

90. Pyrrhus Was Crowned King of Sicily

Pyrrhus then invaded Apulia and attacked the Romans under Gaius Fabricius and Publius Decius Mus, the son of Publius Decius Mus who was consul in 312 BC. The initial battle was long and bloody but, by nightfall, inconclusive. The following day, Pyrrhus with a reputed 70,000 men was, according to Plutarch, able to deploy his nineteen elephants, which then went on to crush, literally, the Roman opposition: the Romans lost 6,000 men, and Pyrrhus some 4,000. According to Dionysius, the Romans tried, unsuccessfully, to stop the elephants by deploying hastily devised anti-elephant devices: troops letting loose salvoes of javelins at the elephants and wagons carrying jibs with burning grappling hooks. The elephants prevailed and furiously attacked the Romans – according to Plutarch the Romans compared their charge to an earthquake or a tsunami, concluding that a discrete retreat was the better part of valour. Livy, however, says that the battle was inconclusive. Dio records that Pyrrhus was defeated while Orosius has it that it was a disaster for Pyrrhus.

Whatever the true outcome, Pyrrhus realised that his costly victories had reduced his army quite considerably and that his resources were diminishing rapidly. After the battles of Heraclea and Asculum he turned to the Romans for a diplomatic solution. Not surprisingly, his condition that the Romans give up any ambitions on the cities of southern Italy was rejected by the Senate, led by Appius Claudius. A later, diminished demand that the Greek cities be merely granted independence from Rome was similarly rejected. It was at this point that the Carthaginians moved in. They were concerned that Pyrrhus was now eying their island of Sicily and so offered naval and financial support to Rome in the hope that this would enable them to prolong their war with Pyrrhus and so deflect him from Sicily.

The Carthaginians were not wrong. After Asculum, Pyrrhus envisaged richer pickings from Sicily, where he had been invited by Syracuse to dispel the Carthaginians. His crossing in the Straits of Messina was attacked by the Carthaginian navy, resulting in the loss of seventy or so of his 110 ships. He was, nevertheless, crowned king of Sicily and in 277 BC captured the Carthaginian stronghold of Eryx – modern Erice. This success persuaded other Greek cities under Carthaginian rule on the island to join him. Negotiations with the Carthaginians began the following year. They were ready to supply Pyrrhus with money and ships but, in accordance with what was agreed with Syracuse, he demanded that Carthage leave Sicily completely. The Greek cities were against peace with Carthage because they still held the strategic stronghold of Lilybaeum (Marsala). Pyrrhus ceded to them and broke off the Carthaginian peace negotiations. His tyrannical attitude, however, and the rough-handed way he treated the Greeks, not least when recruiting oarsmen for his undermanned ships, began to lose him support.

Eryx is built on the summit of Mount Erice, some 750 metres above sea level. Aelian records that animals selected for sacrifice would voluntarily walk up to the temple altar to be slain.

91. Pyrrhus Laid Seige to Fortress Lilybaeum

Pyrrhus then laid siege to fortress Lilybaeum, but after two months realised he needed to blockade the fortress from the sea as well as from land. Pyrrhus then requested troops and money from the Greek cities to enable him to build a fleet. The Greeks refused; Pyrrhus exacted compulsory contributions and set up a military dictatorship with garrisons in the Greek cities. The Greeks were so enraged by this that they were willing to parley with the Carthaginians, who promptly attacked Pyrrhus – unsuccessfully. Pyrrhus had had enough and returned to Italy on the pretext of aiding Tarentum, again in trouble from a coalition of Samnites, Bruttians and Lucanians. As his boat left the island he remarked presciently, 'What a wrestling ground we are leaving, my friends, for the Carthaginians and the Romans.'

The Carthaginians attacked again in the Straits of Messina, inflicting heavy losses on Pyrrhus' fleet. The Mamertines, sons of Mars who inhabited the lands around the straits, anticipated Pyrrhus by crossing ahead of him with an army of 10,000 men. They then proceeded to harry him. Pyrrhus took a blow to the head in one of the skirmishes but responded to a challenge from one of the Mamertines, a giant of a soldier, for one-to-one combat. Pyrrhus squared up to him and delivered a blow to the head that cleaved him clean in half from head to foot – according to Plutarch, the giant literally fell apart. Pyrrhus then continued to Tarentum.

The Mamertines were Italian mercenaries who had been recruited from their home in Campania by Agathocles (361–289 BC), tyrant of Syracuse and self-proclaimed king of Sicily. After Syracuse lost the Third Sicilian War, the city of Messana was given to Carthage in

307 BC. When Agathocles died in 289 BC, many of his mercenaries remained redundant in Sicily. Most of them returned home but some remained and played a major role in the lead up to the First Punic War.

Messana was a crossing point between Italy and Sicily. The inhabitants allowed the Mamertines into their homes; in time the visitors conspired to capture the town. One night, the mercenaries killed most of the population and claimed Messana. The surviving Messanians were thrown out and the properties and women divided up.

In 275 the two Roman armies were in Samnite Beneventum under Manius Curius Dentatus while the other was in Lucania. Pyrrhus sent a unit to preoccupy the latter while he attacked Dentatus with his main force. Pyrrhus' circuitous route under cover of night to attack the Roman camp was exposed when dawn broke, enabling Dentatus to defeat one of Pyrrhus's wings. However, Pyrrhus' elephants were active on the other wing; Dentatus was able to turn them with a salvo of javelins so that they trampled their own men as they fled in panic. Pyrrhus then returned to Epirus and home, leaving Rome victorious and with the Carthaginians to deal with.

92. CROSS-DRESSING AGNODICE WAS THE FIRST PROFESSIONAL MIDWIFE OF ANCIENT GREECE

Agnodice was reputedly the first professional midwife of ancient Greece, practising around 500 BC. As a native of Athens where it was illegal for women or slaves to study or practice medicine, Agnodice was forced to dress as a man while attending medical lectures. On qualifying, women rejected her (as a man) until she revealed that she was a woman. She then incurred the wrath of the Areopagus, who accused her of corrupting her patients, and was charged with practicing illegally. Influential Athenian ladies protested and had the law abolished, after which women were permitted to practice medicine, and to be paid for it.

Many doctors in Rome were Greek-trained doctors. The first Greek physician to go to Rome to practice, Archagathos, arrived around 219. He was an experienced battlefield surgeon, originally called 'the wound healer' (*vulnerarius*) but later earned the sobriquet *carnifex*, the butcher – this probably says as much about the suspicion in which he was held as a foreigner as it does about his surgical expertise. Aulus Cornelius Celsus, the first-century encyclopaedist compiled his *de Medicina*, a work in eight parts covering *the History of Medicine, General Pathology, Specific Diseases, Parts of the Body, Pharmacology, Surgery and Orthopedics*. Alexander Philalethes authored another *Gynaecology*.

Asclepiades of Bithynia (*c.* 120 BC–*c.* 70 BC) arrived and with him an untypically good bedside manner: he practised medicine '*tuto, celerites ac iucunde*' – safely, swiftly and with a smile. Allegedly, he had raised a man from the dead; he repudiated much of the Hippocratic teachings, was admired by Cicero and Lucretius but was later considered a charlatan by Galen. When Julius

Caesar was fatally stabbed, a doctor, Antistius, was called to perform a postmortem in what may be history's first recorded example of a pathologist assisting in a murder case – only one of Caesar's twenty-three stab wounds had proved fatal. In 46 BC Caesar had moved things forward for the profession when he granted Roman citizenship to immigrant doctors working in Rome; in Ephesus doctors were immune from tax, as was Antonius Musa when he shot to fame after curing Augustus of a serious illness with a form of hydrotherapy in 23 BC. Gaius Stertinius Xenophon is another example of a doctor made good. He came from Cos to become court physician to Claudius. He also ran a lucrative practice in Baiae where he financed new public buildings including a library.

The Greek physician Pedanius Dioscorides (*c.* 40-*c.* AD 90) came to Rome during Nero's reign; he was also an accomplished botanist and pharmacologist. Dioscorides stressed the importance of experiential medicine, testing and retesting, and the value of the postmortem examination. His five-volume book *De Materia Medica* is our first pharmacopeia, comprising 1,000 or so natural drugs, nearly 5,000 medicinal applications for drugs, and 360 medical properties for agents such as antiseptics, anti-inflammatories and stimulants. Plants and minerals used specifically by women are recorded, particularly in skin lotions, depilatories, perfumes, even love potions.

93. Archimedes Of Syracuse: One of the Greatest Mathematicians, Physicists, Engineers, Inventors, and Astronomers of All Time

He anticipated calculus and was a leading light in geometry, including discoveries relating to the area of a circle, the surface area and volume of a sphere, and the area under a parabola. He gave an accurate approximation of pi and pioneered the application of mathematics to physical phenomena, founding hydrostatics and statics, including an explanation of how a lever works. The hydraulic (Archimedes') screw (for raising water from a lower to higher level still very much in use in some developing countries), compound pulleys, and innovative war machines were all developed by Archimedes. The law of hydrostatics, 'Archimedes' principle', states that a body immersed in fluid loses weight equal to the weight of the amount of fluid it displaces. Archimedes allegedly discovered this when getting into his bath, causing him to exclaim 'Eureka!' – 'I've got it!' We have all been having 'eureka moments' ever since.

Plutarch gives us this description of just how obsessed Archimedes was and how passionate he was about his work: 'being perpetually charmed by his familiar siren, that is, by his geometry, he neglected to eat and drink and took no care of his person; that he was often carried by force to the baths, and when there he would trace geometrical figures in the ashes of the fire, and with his finger draws lines upon his body when it was anointed with oil, being in a state of great ecstasy and divinely possessed by his science'.

Nine treatises by Archimedes survive: *On the Sphere and Cylinder*; *Measurement of the Circle* gives an approximation of π (pi); *On Conoids and Spheroids* determines the volumes of the segments of solids formed by the revolution of a conic section (circle, ellipse, parabola, or hyperbola) about its axis; *On Spirals* develops many properties of tangents to, and areas associated with, the spiral of Archimedes; *On the Equilibrium of Planes* establishes the 'law of the lever'; *Quadrature of the Parabola*; *The Sand-Reckoner* is written for the layman and computes the number of grains of sand that will fit inside the universe; *Method Concerning Mechanical Theorems* describes his discoveries in mathematics; *On Floating Bodies* is the first known work on hydrostatics; *Archimedes' Cattle Problem* in which Archimedes challenges mathematicians in Alexandria to count the numbers of cattle in the Herd of the Sun by solving a number of simultaneous Diophantine equations: the answer is approximately $7.760271 \times 10^{206544}$.

In 1973 the Archimedes heat ray was put to the test by Greek scientist Ioannis Sakkas. Seventy mirrors were used around 5 by 3 feet each with a copper coating. The mirrors were pointed at a plywood mock-up of a Roman warship 160 feet away. When the mirrors were focused, the ship burst into flames within a few seconds. The plywood ship had a coating of tar paint, which may have helped combustion, but tar would have been usual on ships of the time.

94. The Accidental Death of Archimedes is One of History's Most Notorious Cases of Mistaken Identity

The killing of Archimedes at the end of the siege of Syracuse (213–211 BC) is one of history's most notorious cases of mistaken identity.

King Hiero II of Syracuse (r. 270 to 215 BC) had been a long-standing ally of the Romans from 263 BC, but his death in 215 BC led to the accession of his naive grandson, Hieronymous. Hieronymous was taken in by an offer from Rome's arch-enemy Carthage of half of Sicily in return for his military support, but he was assassinated and his policy in relation to Rome was reversed. The Carthaginians put out propaganda that the Romans, under Claudius Marcellus, had taken Leontini and sacked and pillaged it somewhat overzealously. The Syracusans responded by butchering a number of Romans and renewing their alliance with Carthage. Marcellus resorted to damage limitation by laying siege to Syracuse by land and by sea. But Syracuse, the most beautiful of Greek colonial cities, was well prepared: Hiero had installed catapults that outranged the Roman artillery, and a formidable array of anti-siege machinery. This was the war work of Archimedes, a Syracusan citizen on a sabbatical from less bellicose studies, now focusing on inventing military machinery.

Eventually Marcellus took the city and allowed his troops to sack and plunder it: one of the victims was Archimedes, run through by a legionary despite specific orders to spare him. When he burst in, the soldier asked him who he was as he poured over his plans and diagrams – but Archimedes asked not to be disturbed. Patience was in short supply, and Archimedes' instruments looked like good booty: the Roman slew him. Archimedes' last words were 'Do not disturb my circles' ('μή μου τοὺς κύκλους τάραττε'), or, in Latin: *Noli turbare circulos meos*. Nothing in this riddle suggested to the soldier that he was confronting the protected Archimedes.

Archimedes himself was an invaluable secret weapon. His military inventions include the 'claw' and the heat ray – both born out of necessity during the vicissitudes of the siege of Syracuse. The claw of Archimedes, also known as 'the ship shaker', comprised a crane-like arm with a metal grappling hook on the end; the claw would be dropped onto a ship, lifting it out of the water, dropping it back in and, in all probability, sinking it.

As for the heat ray, Archimedes used mirrors as a parabolic reflector to burn ships attacking Syracuse. 'Archimedes' heat ray' simply focused sunlight onto enemy ships, setting them on fire. This resulted from his interest in catoptrics, the branch of optics dealing with the reflection of light from mirrors, plane or curved.

Archimedes also gets the credit for improving the power and accuracy of the catapult, and with inventing the odometer during the First Punic War. The odometer was described as a cart with a gear mechanism that dropped a ball into a container after each mile traveled.

95. The First Macedonian War Was Indecisive; the Second Macedonian War Less So

The First Macedonian War was indecisive: it merely showcased the expansionist ambitions of Philip V of Macedon who signed an alliance with Hannibal after Cannae, perhaps with an eye to invading southern Italy in the footsteps of Pyrrhus.

The second war opened with the Battle of Athacus. This came about after Rome agreed to help the Rhodians and Attalus against an increasingly aggressive Philip. The Romans had flatly rejected a request for armed assistance from the Aetolian League the previous year, due to war weariness and commitments in the western Mediterranean. This situation had not changed in 200 BC, so it seems likely that they agreed now because they knew of the clandestine alliance between Philip and Antiochus III – and because they were alarmed by an attack on Athens by the Acarnanians, allies of Philip. The Romans may have been overawed by Antiochus after his recently concluded invasion of India, or, more precisely, the Kabul Valley, and his victory over Bactria and Parthia. On his own he may not have posed a threat, but in an alliance with Philip he was considerably more worrying.

Philip attacked Athens again and moved into what is now the Dardanelles, laying siege to Abydus; here his reputation for barbaric cruelty preceded him. He announced to the inhabitants that the walls were about to be stormed and that anyone contemplating suicide (to avoid the rapine of his troops) should do so within three days. The Abydans, fearing the worst, killed all their women and children and threw all their goods and possessions into the sea. All the remaining men fought until the end.

Philip rejected an ultimatum from Rome, which insisted he indemnify Rhodes and Pergamum and desist from any action against any Greek state. Sulpicius Galba then landed in Illyria with a modest force of 30,000 men conveyed by an equally modest fleet, and moved east into Macedonia. The two armies met head on but the battle was inconclusive.

Two years later the Romans were back in Greece under the consul Titus Quinctius Flamininus, who invaded Macedonia. After some weeks' delay, Philip sued for peace but the Roman terms were so exacting that continuing the war was the only option. Flamininus eyed the Macedonian catapults lining the ravine of the River Aous with some trepidation and concern. The day was saved, however, by a turncoat shepherd who agreed to take the Romans safely down the river to emerge at the rear of the enemy. On arrival they attacked; Philip fled on hearing the clamour of more Romans converging from behind. In the meantime Flaminius secured the support of the Aetolians and the Achaean League. The Roman again resorted to diplomacy but Philip rejected terms that entailed surrendering his three 'Fetters of Greece': Demetrias, Chalcis and Acrocorinth.

Flamininus, a philhellene, was much more proactive than Galba had been, insisting that Philip renounce his claim to the Greek cities and stay within Macedon: peace in Greece and liberty for the Greeks were his watchwords.

96. The Battles of Cynoscephalae and Thermopylae Were Decisive

The decisive battle of the war came the following year at Cynoscephalae. After a number of minor skirmishes, the 25,000 Macedonians, strengthened by 6,000 Aetolians, charged the Romans, inflicting heavy casualties. Flamininus rallied, however, and returned the favour by successfully deploying his elephants and his infantry; a military tribune made the decisive move when he fortuitously detached two maniples and brought them to bear at the Macedonians' rear. The Romans lost 700 men that day; the Macedonians 13,000. Philip asked for a ceasefire; peace was signed in 196. Philip's son was sent to Rome as a hostage.

Greece was now Rome's. Nevertheless, the Romans kept garrisons in the strategic Macedonian cities that had belonged to Macedon – Corinth, Chalcis and Demetrias. Rome had succeeded in its pretext for war, its spurious *casus belli*: defending the freedom of the Greek cities. When Flaminius announced the freedom of the Greek cities at the Isthmian Games in Corinth in 196, he received an ovation the like of which had never been given – even to a Greek. The Romans finally withdrew from Greece in 194 BC, evidence that Rome had no expansionist intentions there.

Over on the other side of the Mediterranean the Aetolian League was feeling aggrieved at the settlement they received following the Second Macedonian War. They had been Rome's allies and were hoping to annex all of Thessaly under the terms of the peace agreement, but they received considerably less. Accordingly, they enlisted the support of Antiochus III ostensibly to help them liberate Greece from the Romans. Antiochus, elevated to commander in chief of the Aetolian League, landed in Thessaly at Demetrias with 10,000 men and overran it. However, he found no Greek support; he and the Aetolians were on their own and the Romans, concerned lest Antiochus had designs on Italy, were advancing under Manius Acilius Glabro with an army of 20,000 men and a squadron of elephants. Philip V entered into an alliance with the Romans. Antiochus retreated to Thermopylae where the Aetolians manned the mountains above the pass. Marcus Cato and Lucius Valerius attacked them. The victorious Cato then charged down the pass causing Antiochus to flee with the loss of nearly his entire army. Antiochus then returned to Asia leaving the Aetolians to sort out the mess.

Glabro demanded unconditional surrender, which the Aetolians refused. The resulting war was cut short by L. Cornelius Scipio, the brother of Africanus and consul for 190 BC, who offered an armistice so that the legions could be deployed against Antiochus in Asia Minor. Marcus Fulvius Nobilior then reduced the Aetolian League to virtual impotence with his treaty confining the members to their borders and stipulating they have the same allies and enemies as Rome. The Romans pulled out in 188 BC. Seventeen years of peace in Greece followed.

97. Perseus Antagonised the Romans by Invading Thessaly

Hostilities resumed against the Macedonians in 171 BC. Philip had spent the last seventeen years peacefully strengthening his country economically and politically: reinforcing his borders, exploiting mineral resources, introducing new taxation and settling Thracians in Macedonia to ease a manpower problem. Philip had two sons – Perseus and Demetrias. Demetrias built up strong diplomatic relations in Rome, so all augured well for the future. Perseus, however, saw this as complicating his own designs to succeed his father and had his brother executed on spurious charges of treason. Philip was plagued by guilt and planned to disinherit Perseus, but it was too late. Perseus acceded to the throne on Philip's death in 179 BC. Initially cautious, Perseus carried on his father's good work but he was always viewed with suspicion by Rome. His marriage to Laodice, daughter of Seleucus IV of Syria (successor to Antiochus III) and his sister Apame's marriage to Prusias II of Bythinia did not help, nor did the fact that his pro-Roman neighbours were spying on him, spinning everything with an anti-Perseus twist. Most active was Eumenes III of ever-hostile Pergamum, who turned up at Rome and delivered a character assassination of Perseus in person. This, and the translation of suspicions into belligerent action, led to a declaration of war in which the Macedonians, thanks to the prudent domestic war preparations by Philip and Perseus, saw them field an army of some 40,000 men and 4,000 cavalry.

Perseus antagonized the Romans by invading Thessaly and setting up a garrison at Mount Othrys. Publius Licinius Crassus marched to meet him from Epirus and camped at Larissa with 30,000 men in total. After several days' procrastination, the two armies clashed at Callinicus in what was to be a disaster of the first magnitude for the Romans. They lost 3,000 men to the Macedonians' sixty. Perseus offered peace but the Romans flatly rejected it.

The Romans restored some of their pride later that year at Phalanna when they were attacked by Perseus while out foraging. The tribune, Lucius Pompeius, withdrew to a hill where he was besieged by the Macedonians. Crassus relieved his colleague and proceeded to rout Perseus' forces. The loss of 8,000 dead and 3,000 taken prisoner was enough to make Perseus retreat back into Macedonia.

98. USCANA, SCODRA, PYTHIUM AND PYDNA SAW THE END OF THE THIRD MACEDONIAN WAR

Another disaster was waiting for the Romans at Uscanian, Illyria. Appius Claudius Cento opposed a force led by Gentius, king of the Illyrians, now an ally of Macedonia. Claudius fell for a trap in which the inhabitants of Uscana pretended to be willing to betray their city to him. As Claudius approached what he believed to be an empty city, his army was overcome by a charge of the inhabitants. Only half of Claudius' 4,000 men escaped with their lives. In 168 BC, Gentius was attacked in his capital, Scodra, captured and taken to Rome. Two years later Aemilius Paullus faced Perseus across the Elpeus, a dried-up river that was impossible to cross. He sent Scipio Nasica with 8,000 infantry and 120 cavalry ostensibly to the coastal town of Heracleum but really in the opposite direction to Pythium, the sanctuary of Apollo on Mount Olympus. Perseus could still see Paulus and was quite unaware of Scipio's position until a deserter revealed the plan. Perseus sent 2,000 Macedonians with 10,000 mercenaries after Scipio. Scipio, however, overcame the Macedonians, who fled. Perseus withdrew to Pydna.

The battle-hardened Aemilius Paullus joined Scipio at Pydna to confront Perseus. Allegedly, Paullus caused a horse to bolt and thus triggered the start of the one-hour afternoon conflict. In a battle reminiscent of Cynoscephalae, the consul exploited gaps in the Macedonian centre, causing them to discard their long, unwieldy pikes and depend on their short swords in the close combat that followed. The flexible maniples and the use of tempered steel as opposed to iron won the day for the Romans. Perseus fled in the rout that followed leaving 25,000 Macedonians dead; he later surrendered and brought the Third Macedonian War to an end. All royal officials were excommunicated while Perseus was detained in virtual house arrest in Alba Fucens. On a wider scale, the Romans carried out a rigorous and ruthless purge of inconvenient Greek citizens, many of them denounced by neighbours and friends of Rome.

In 150 BC a pretender to the Macedonian throne, Andriscus, claimed to be a son of Perseus. In what became known as the Fourth Macedonian War, Andriscus defeated a small Roman force despatched to deal with him. Success was short-lived, however, as a second army in 148 BC under Quintus Cacilius Metellus expelled him from Macedonia, catching up with him in Thrace. This minor war was important because it brought it home to the Romans that, politically, something more robust and permanent was required of them in Greece. Accordingly, Macedonia became a Roman province, incorporating Thessaly and Epirus. The Via Egnatia was built, leading from Apollonia to Thessalonica and remained the only decent road in Albania until the Italian invasion in 1916.

99. The Gymnasium Was *the* Place to Go

One of *the* places to go for the well-to-do Greek in a city or town of any size was the gymnasium. The word is from γυμνός, *gymnós* meaning naked, and then the verb γυμνάζω (*gymnazo*), to train naked, train in gymnastic exercise, or simply to train, to exercise. The local gymnasium was a place where a man could work out, preen, bathe, meet friends and conduct homosexual affairs if he so wished. It was also the training place for contestants in local and national athletic games. Attached to the gymnasium was the *palaestra* (παλαίστρα), the wrestling and boxing school. The *dromos*, or running track, was the other main feature. Military training took place there too. There were horse and chariot race tracks, and baths and shops selling athletic accoutrements.

The gymnasia were state-controlled and open to all freeborn males; they were under the supervision of gymnasiarchs – public officials responsible for the running of sports and games at public festivals. The *gymnastai* were the teachers, coaches, and trainers of the athletes.

Gymnasia soon became inextricably connected with education through the recognition by the Greeks of the strong relation between athletics, education and health. Physical training and health maintenance were salient features of a child's early education, and the education of young men largely took place in the gymnasium, where provision was made, for example, for instruction in morals and ethics. This, of course, meant that gymnasia were frequented by teachers and philosophers.

There were three great public gymnasia in Athens: the Academy, the Lyceum and the Cynosarges. Each was associated with a famous school of philosophy: Antisthenes founded a school at the Cynosarges, from which our word Cynic derives. Plato founded a school at the Academy, and at the Lyceum, Aristotle founded the Peripatetic school.

Athens had ten gymnasiarchs who were appointed annually – one from each tribe. They looked after and compensated athletes training for public contests, ran the games at the Athenian festivals, and decorated and maintained the gymnasium. Reporting to them were ten s*ophronistae* responsible for the conduct of the athletes.

Paedotribae and *gymnastae* were responsible for coaching methods; the *gymnastae* also took care of the health of the pupils and prescribed remedies when they became unwell. The *aleiptae* oiled and dusted the bodies of the youths, acted as doctors, and administered any drugs prescribed.

In 1859 *The Atlantic* described gymnastics as follows: 'Two distinct yet harmonious branches of study claimed the early attention of the youth of ancient Greece. Education was comprised in the two words, Music and Gymnastics. Plato includes it all under these divisions:--"That having reference to the body is gymnastics, but to the cultivation of the mind, music."... Grammar, Music, and Gymnastics, then, comprised the whole curriculum of study which was prescribed to the Athenian boy. There were not separate and distinct learned professions, or faculties, to so great an extent as in modern times... The young grow most in height and can best gain an harmonious development by frequenting the GYMNASIUM.' (http://www.theatlantic.com/magazine/archive/1859/05/the gymnasium/305407/)

100. The Achaean War: Rome Gained Hegemony over All of Greece

In view of the decidedly loose control under which the Romans left the Greek towns and cities, it was hardly surprising when a dispute arose after Rome's deportation of 1,000 Achaean citizens to Rome after the Third Macedonian War. Naturally, the Achaean League protested, but their citizens remained incarcerated without trial for fifteen years. Of the total, 700 died as a result of the conditions of their confinement; the survivors were released in 150 BC but too late to moderate the anger felt by the Achaeans. Corinth was particularly militant and appointed a dictator, Critolaus, who, in 146, invaded central Greece. He was, however, defeated by Caecilius Metellus at the Alpheus River. Florus is mistaken when he says that this ended the Achaean War.

Undeterred, Critolaus then attacked Heraclea, a town which had declined the offer to join the Achaean League. Once again, Critolaus was soundly beaten by Metellus and took refuge in Scarphea; he was never heard of again. A force of 1,000 Arcadians, on its way to reinforce Critolaus, was also massacred by Metellus.

Diaeus replaced Critolaus and raised an army of 14,000 infantry and 600 cavalry; 4,000 were sent to garrison Megara but these fled to Corinth on the approach of an army under Lucius Mummius – 23,000 foot and 3,500 horse. The Achaean cavalry fled the field leaving their infantry to its fate. Mummius then proceeded remorselessly to sack and raze what was a virtually deserted gem of a city. There is some mitigation in the fact that many of the exquisite works of art were shipped back to Rome before the bonfires were lit. The men were killed while the women and children were sold as slaves. The Achaean League was disbanded, its towns absorbed into the province of Macedonia; Corinth was erased as an example and in order to prevent it becoming a future commercial rival to Rome. Its captured inhabitants were sold off into slavery. Weapons and armour throughout the region were seized and local militia activity was outlawed. Mummius received the *agnomen* Achaichus in recognition of his victory over the Achaean League. Julius Caesar refounded the city as *Colonia Laus Iulia Corinthiensis*, Colony of Corinth in Praise of Julius, in 44 BC just before his assassination.

Rome gained hegemony over all of Greece. But while Greek culture and influence persisted for centuries to come, the ancient Greeks, in all their manifestations, became part of the burgeoning empire of Roman conquests in the Mediterranean world and far beyond.

Corinth rivaled Athens and Thebes and until the mid-sixth century was a major exporter of black-figure pottery to city-states around the Greek world. Corinth had a temple of Aphrodite, employing around a thousand temple prostitutes who served the wealthy merchants and the powerful officials who frequented the city. Lais, the most famous *hetaira*, was reputed to charge extortionate fees for her favours.